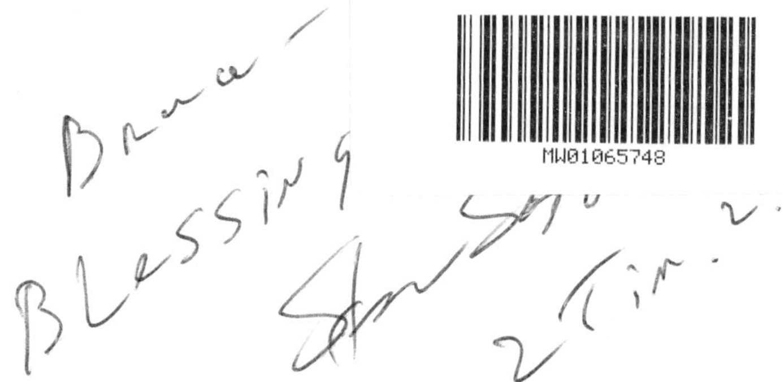

Today's WORD on Money™

"Outside-the-Box, Inside-the-Kingdom" Wealth Principles

By Steven P. Sappington

First Edition – December 2010

ISBN
978-1-77067-257-4 (Hardcover)
978-1-77067-258-1 (Paperback)
978-1-77067-259-8 (eBook)

Published by:

FriesenPress
Suite 300 – 852 Fort Street
Victoria, BC, Canada V8W 1H8

www.friesenpress.com

For information on bulk orders contact:
info@friesenpress.com or fax 1-888-376-7026

Distributed to the trade by The Ingram Book Company

Table of Contents

HOLIDAY TOPICS:

ENDORSEMENTS

"Money is not a problem, but it is a symptom of so many personal, relational, and spiritual issues we face in our lives. We don't have a money problem. We have a knowledge and wisdom problem. Books like Today's WORD on Money are important as we seek the information that will help us manage our money instead of allowing our money to manage us."
Jim Stovall, Author, The Ultimate Gift

"In the midst of tremendous financial uncertainty, the most certain thing we have is our faith that the Father is for us so who can be against us. The 40 day challenge that Steve has laid out for us may well be the best use of our time, our energy and our focus. These meditations will not change our circumstances, but they will change us; in a way that may well change the financial circumstances affecting our lives. Steve has presented us with the word of God in a powerful and challenging way. Read it for 40 days and be blessed."
Alan Ross, CEO of Kingdom Companies.

"Steve Sappington is a man who practices what he preaches. He has put together a book of meditations that will enrich anyone's life. I am delighted to be able to endorse Steve and his book. I am hoping that this will be used by thousands and thousands of people."
Ron Blue, President of Kingdom Advisors

"Steve offers up an easy-to-understand guide to money management with Today's WORD on Money™. The words are down—to—earth, but divinely inspired. Almost any question you can think of relating to finances and life are covered. Read it. You will be better prepared for what's ahead."
Tim Wildmon, President, American Family Association

"Steve Sappington is my financial advisor, and these 40 daily devotions will provide you with wise, biblically based counsel on financial matters. Steve's approach is to seek God's will with financial resources and let Him lead towards successful stewardship and investment. Today's WORD on Money™ provides biblical guidance on how to best use your gifts and resources. These daily devotions will be a blessing to you and those you advise or mentor."
Ian McCaw, Director of Athletics, Baylor University

"The quality of life is dependent upon your spiritual, moral and ethical values to establish priorities. Financial investments are a necessary part of personal stewardship and should reflect those same values. Steve does a remarkable job in emphasizing those values as he discusses the different types of appropriate investment opportunities. This book is a profitable reading experience."
B. Joe Cline, CFM, Vice President - Private Investments - Merrill Lynch (Retired)

"Steve Sappington has written a wonderful treatise on how to live. I recommend his book to all who yearn for a deeper meaning to our existence on this earth."
R. Nelson Nash, Author, Becoming Your Own Banker

"Steve Sappington has hit the nail on the head! A much needed resource! In a world of financial ambiguity and questionable advice, Steve provides sound, Biblical wisdom with highly practical, actionable insight that can help anyone get on a solid financial footing and plan well for their golden years."
Michael Pink, Founder, Michael Pink Innovations

"Today's WORD on Money™ is a must read because it addresses a core issue that we all struggle with every day – how we deal with money and possessions. Tell me how someone deals with money

and possessions and I will tell you the depth of that person's relationship with the Lord who created the Universe. Steve Sappington has hit the nail on the head in his book. The Bible speaks more about money and possessions than almost any topic. This book will liberate those who are held captive by a wrong understanding of money and possessions and will provide wise counsel on how best to manage what God has entrusted to us to advance His Kingdom."
Mathew D. Staver, Founder and Chairman, Liberty Counsel; Dean and Professor of Law, Liberty University School of Law

----

"Through daily instruction, scripture reading, meditation, and paradigm shifters, Today's WORD on Money™ is a much needed resource for understanding our financial obligations and stewardship. Integrating faith with personal financial planning, Steve Sappington writes with refreshing candor, presenting otherwise complex issues clearly and practically. I encourage you to learn what the Word says about money and follow the advice in this valuable book."
David Wesley Whitlock, President, Oklahoma Baptist University

----

"Through illuminating Biblical principles and wisdom, the paradigm shifts found in Today's WORD on Money™ are sure to bring healing to our financially injured culture."
J. Scott Wieters, MD FAAEM

"Steve gives us practical, countercultural financial wisdom in bite sized pieces. Share this gold mine of biblical insights with your children and close friends, and they will be forever grateful."
Kent Humphreys, FCCI / Christ@Work

"Dear Steve,
What a timely expository on the power, purpose and God's plan for money.
Very sincerely yours,
Richard Weylman," www.richardweylman.com

"Steve has done an excellent job explaining financial concepts within a radical theology and philosophy of stewardship. And it is presented in a format that is not only easy to accommodate, but also to assimilate into a giving lifestyle. This should move any reader a step closer to receiving that *hug from the father* when He says, '*Well done, thou good and faithful servant.*'"
Ray Lyne, Founder of **Lifestyle Giving, Inc.**

"Steve,
We're so thankful that the Lord has guided you to write such a clear-cut, readily accessible, biblical view of God's way to manage His resources. The Scriptures you included for thought and study are packed with potential for growth for anyone wanting to learn more about stewardship. We fully support your writing and look forward to the next installment."
Frank & Linda Fyke (Steve's church "Life Group" leaders)

"Finally someone has done it! Someone has written a book about God's laws of finance and investment that a lay person like me can understand. Steve Sappington's book, "Today's Word on Money" is that book. For years, sitting in a financial adviser's office was like sitting in a doctor's office. I didn't understand half of what they were saying. Having read this book, I feel like Hank Williams and can say, 'Praise the Lord, I see the light.' It is a must for every person who wants to learn God's Biblical principles of money management. I recommend it highly."
Barry Camp, Senior Pastor, Highland Baptist Church, Waco, TX

"Early in this book, Steve wisely points out that financial remedies are of little value without the proper heart. While valuable to everyone, the words and exercises of this book will be especially valuable for those with a heart that is seeking God."
Leo Wells, President and Founder, Wells Real Estate Funds, Inc.

"Steve Sappington is a man of integrity and purity. His desire to share truth that transforms and empowers people has not only helped me and my family but has touched thousands of lives. I look so forward to the fresh truths that Steve has written and know that it will be a blessing to all."
Jimmy Seibert, Senior Pastor, Antioch Community Church

"The scripture's teachings about money are really lessons about life. Steve makes this abundantly clear in Today's WORD on Money. From the beginning the matters of life, faith and finances are framed in the context of the heart and if one reads and applies the truths found in this book, they will have their heart, mind and stewardship impacted for the benefit of this world and the next. Thank you, Steve, for bringing a clear and fresh perspective to these most important topics."
David Wills, President, National Christian Foundation

"Steve Sappington has reminded us that wisdom, even regarding challenging subjects, need not be complex. Clarity regarding the value and purpose of money often eludes financial professionals, but Steve has addressed the subject in a way that is clear and compelling for all of us who need a reminder of the importance and usefulness of simple truths."
David Sallee, President, William Jewell College

"Having managed money for clients over the past 2 decades, I have found that companies whose leaders try to 'cut corners' or in some way circumvent moral and ethical behavior will eventually fail and/or lose money for their investors. Today's WORD on Money™ gives valuable guidelines for those who want to avoid such failures by conducting their personal, financial and business affairs in line with Biblical principles."
Paul Dietrich, Chairman, CEO, and Co-Chief Investment Officer, Foxhall Capital Management, Inc.

"Having known Steve and valuing his sound opinions, it was refreshing for me to read Today's WORD on Money™. In these times of fast moving business conditions and ever changing investment markets, I feel that an honest and clear point of view, based on integrity and solid spiritual values is essential. Steve provides this perspective in this practical guide to personal finance. Those of us wanting a true long term financial plan need to read this book.
Eugene E. Ellison, CLU, ChFC

Steve's book is exemplary and is timely and needed in these current economic times. Steve writes powerfully about the need for holiness. One measure of the impact of a book is what it causes one to think and act as a result of reading it. This book should inspire people to cultivate a deeper relationship with God in all facets of our lives. It is a much needed practical guide and encouragement to people who want to succeed by applying biblical prospects to all areas of financial planning. This book is for the people who strive for integrity and completeness with God in all areas of life. With God all is holy.
Al Hartman, CEO Hartman Income REIT, Inc.

Today's WORD on Money™ provides a refreshing perspective on finances that is greatly needed and seldom emphasized in our impulsive society. The solid principles presented will help you align your fiscal purposes with God's eternal Word and orient your life toward the Savior. Regardless of your personal financial situation you will find TWOM to be an extremely valuable resource!
Alton Jones, 2008 Bassmaster Classic World Champion

"This timely book combines common sense, research, and academics, but the important message is based upon guiding principles inspired some 2000 years ago."
Don Powell, 18th Chairman of FDIC, Former Federal Coordinator of Gulf Coast Rebuilding

----

Having taught many on how to conduct their business based on Biblical Principles, I'm always amazed at how well meaning Christians live segmented lives and unknowingly put other priorities and traditions ahead of the very God they profess to worship. I have been guilty of this very thing. Given the drastic changes in our economy and the constant market instability, we now more than ever need prophets and teachers who will take us back to basics on the root cause of our corporate and individual dilemmas in an uncompromising way. *Today's Word on Money*™ is more than just a book of information and strategies on money and wealth, but it is rather a revelatory and transformational book that speaks to the most important aspect of our lives: our total being and our attitude about finances and everything we possess. It is applicable today, tomorrow and yesterday. It is founded on unchanging truths, and it is written by someone who has the experience and transparency to relate to each one of us recovering idol worshipers. Make this a part of your library and your life today.
Patrice Tsague, Chief Servant Officer, Nehemiah Project International Ministries, Inc.

Today's WORD on Money™

("Outside-the-Box, Inside-the-Kingdom" Wealth Principles)

"What is 1440?"

There are 1440 minutes in a day. All of us are given the same amount of time. Why do some achieve more than others? The better question is "How are you using the skills, gifts and abilities that God has given specifically to you?" You are uniquely designed and shaped by God. When you compare yourself to others, you miss the point of God's work in you, and you can build envy and jealousy in your heart.

You are a steward, responsible for the 1440 minutes in your day, and for your God-given skills, gifts and abilities. Are you intentional in what you read and put into your mind, in how you spend your time, and in what you think about during the day? If you are not growing, then you are dying: without an investment there is no appreciation.

Another way to say this is that there is no free lunch. Without some sacrifice of labor, time, suffering or expense, there is no appreciation. It is the sacrifice that brings the appreciation. How are you investing
to gain appreciation? What asset do you have that is going up in value? Is your relationship with God appreciating and growing, or is it dying? How much investment have you made in this relationship?

Take the 40 Day Challenge

Do you rush through the day, or are you intentional in recognizing God throughout the day? Jesus said that the greatest commandment is "to love the Lord with ALL of your heart, mind, soul and strength." The greatest asset that you have is your life. How are you investing? Is your life appreciating? The world's system wants us to define assets in temporal and financial terms. God looks at the eternal assets. Are you investing for eternity or for the temporal? Take the challenge and experience the appreciation.

Glenn Repple, CEO and founder of G.A. Repple & Company, www.garepple.com

Acknowledgements

First I acknowledge my Heavenly Father, the King of the Universe, who has mercifully forgiven all my sins and redeemed my life from destruction. I thank my Lord and Savior Jesus Christ who took my place on the cross, thereby purchasing eternal life for me now and forever. And I thank the Holy Spirit who fills me, guides me and protects me.

I am so thankful to my wife Anna, who works harder than any human being I've ever known, and who has taught me so much about how to love God. I am thankful to my children, Wil, Ruth, and Sara for their childlike abilities to overlook all my shortcomings, including the many times that I have spent more time on business than I have with them. I'm thankful to my parents, Richard and Katherine Sappington, for rearing me in a Godly home. And I'm thankful to Jeanette Snow, my junior high English teacher, for teaching me how to diagram sentences.

I thank my Broker-Dealer, Glenn Repple, for continually setting a Godly example for me of what a Biblical Financial Advisor should do and be. I thank my other mentors who have taught me over the years:

Don Blanton of Money*Trax*
Ray Lyne of Lifestyle Giving
Paul J. Meyer, salesman, entrepreneur, author, and philanthropist
Nelson Nash, author of Becoming Your Own Banker
Homer Owen of the Samaritan Foundation
Frank Reynolds of Frank Reynolds Wealth Management
Alan Ross of Kingdom Companies
Patrice Tsague of Nehemiah Project International Ministries

Thanks to those who graciously gave their time to read or make suggestions for this book:

Eric Bahme, Senior Pastor of Eastside Foursquare Church in Portland, Oregon
David Barton, Founder and President of WallBuilders, LLC
Robert Baldwin, President of Christian Care Medi-Share
Ron Blue, President of Kingdom Advisors
David Boren, former U.S. Senator and current President of the University of Oklahoma
Barry Camp, Senior Pastor, Highland Baptist Church in Waco, Texas
Rich Christiano, movie writer, producer, director
B. Joe Cline, CFM, retired Vice President with Merrill Lynch
Richard Cole, Managing Member, Innovasource
Rodney Cox, Ministry Insights
Paul Dietrich, Chairman, CEO, and Co-Chief Investment Officer, Foxhall Capital Management, Inc.
Matthew Deutsch, CPA, The Deutsch Group
Barry Dyke, author of The Pirates of Manhattan,
Gene Ellison, Financial Advisor
Dr. James W. (Bob) Evans, my childhood pastor, retired professor, Oklahoma Baptist University
Linda and Frank Fyke, leaders of my church life group
Bill Garner, independent associate, Pre-Paid Legal Services, Inc.
Ken Goss, owner Goss RV Inc.
Allen Hartman, President of Hartman Management, L.P.
Os Hillman, author, Founder and President of Marketplace Leaders
Kent Humphreys, entrepreneur, Ambassador—Fellowship of Companies for Christ International
Alton Jones, 2008 Bassmaster Classic Champion
Rusty Leonard of Stewardship Partners
Lenny LeBlanc, singer-songwriter, recording artist and worship leader
Greg May, owner of Greg May Honda and Greg May Chevrolet
Ian McCaw, Director of Athletics, Baylor University
Heather Mercer, co-author of Prisoners of Hope
Dayton Molendorp, Chairman, President and CEO of OneAmerica Financial Partners, Inc.
John Mulder, President of WaterStone™
Michael Pink, consultant, author of numerous books, Co-Founder of Michael Pink Innovations

Don Powell, 18th Chairman of FDIC, Former Federal Coordinator of Gulf Coast Rebuilding
John Riddle, author, and my "agent" and editor
Sandy Rios, President of Culture Campaign
Dr. David Sallee, President of William Jewell College
Jimmy Seibert, my pastor, Senior Pastor of Antioch Community Church in Waco
Tom Stansbury, Entrepreneur-in-Residence, Regent University Center for Entrepreneurship
Mat Staver, Founder and Chairman, Liberty Counsel; Dean, Liberty University School of Law
Dan Stratton, author, pastor of Faith Exchange Fellowship, founder of ProVision Network
Kurtis Ward, attorney—Oklahoma City, OK
Leo Wells, Founder and President of Wells Real Estate Funds
Richard Weylman, author, speaker, consultant, coach
Dr. David Whitlock, President of Oklahoma Baptist University
Scott Wieters, M.D., Providence Health Center, Waco, TX
David Wills, President of National Christian Foundation

Foreword

by Paul J. Meyer

Note from Author regarding Paul J. Meyer, who wrote the foreword for Today's WORD on Money™ and passed away in late 2009:

> I first met Mr. Meyer in 1988, when my family and I moved to Waco to work in the Home Office of one of his companies, Success Motivation Institute. Paul formed SMI to "help people reach more of their God-given potential."
>
> Combined sales of programs written by Paul Meyer exceed 3 billion dollars worldwide, more than any other author in this field. He is considered by many to be the founder of the personal development industry.
>
> Paul and his wife Jane, through their family foundation have made gifts approaching $100 million. The purpose of their foundation is to "Do all the good you can, By all the means you can, In all the ways you can, In all the places you can, At all the times you can, To all the people you can, As long as ever you can."
>
> I first emailed Paul about endorsing my book. Paul "kicked it up a notch." Ever the salesman, he offered to help me publish my book through a publishing company that he formed specifically to help first-time authors. But even though I opted for another publisher, Paul still graciously offered to write the foreword for my book. When I re-

ceived the foreword, I told him that I hope someday to write as well as he does.

Steve Sappington's timing couldn't be any better. With the endless stream of reports from media outlets, financial experts, and the government about our nation's gloomy economy, along with the ensuing concern and anxiety, his book, Today's WORD on Money,™ offers a much-needed message of hope and help to those who desire to approach this dismal state of affairs with a more positive attitude and outlook.

Initially, when outlining the topics for the book, Steve considered a straightforward, practical guide to personal financial planning and management. But, while drafting outlines about estate planning, mortgages, and savings and investments, he realized that any remedy, particularly in today's corrupt financial environment, would have little worth without an outright change in personal responsibility. . . a "change of heart," as Steve put it. First, Americans as individuals and then our society as a whole must be really honest about the root of our country's financial ills.

Although his views might be distasteful to some, Steve points to a lack of spirituality as the source of our troubles; he puts the blame squarely at our feet for worshipping false gods . . . the gods of consumerism and greed. That's a tough pill to swallow, but it makes absolute sense. We want to live beyond our means (bigger house than we can afford, more car than we really need, the newest hand-held communication devices, extravagances for our children without the benefit of them earning it, and on and on). And we want these things even if it means we have to dance with the devil!

He isn't saying we should deny ourselves of all comfort and even some luxury, and he certainly isn't suggesting we should live in dreary austerity. He just thinks we've forgotten to put God first in our lives. "As long as we serve the gods of this world it doesn't matter what 'quick fixes' or investment solutions we try," he says. We still will be living a life clouded by half-truths and lies.

In Today's WORD on Money,™ Steve addresses the common topics of financial management, but supports the discussion with fundamental truths from Scripture that shed light on the things we should consider to be most important when making decisions regarding our personal finances.

Steve challenges us to work through the daily lessons, read the accompanying Scripture, and contemplate the daily meditations for 40 days. You are sure to renew your mind, your heart, and especially your spiritual soul, not just during these stormy periods of financial uncertainty, but for all of your life.

And, as Steve points, you have His WORD on it.

Paul J. Meyer
Founder of Success Motivation International Inc.,
and over 40 other companies and
New York Times best-selling author

Preface:

How I Almost Bankrupted My Family

Before I "launch out into the deep" with these lessons, let me preface them by saying this: I am as guilty as anyone of the mistakes I will be discussing. I had originally planned to write a different preface. And the first draft of this book included about 15 additional lessons on topics such as advanced estate design, insurance and several alternative investments. But as I was engrossed in writing information about products and strategies, I suddenly realized that financial remedies are of little value without a change of heart. This has been true in my life, and I believe it is true for America. So we plan to publish our discussion of products in a second book. Also, please bear with me as I "set the stage." This preface may seem "preachy" to some, but please don't tune me out. In the long run, my intent is to uplift and to encourage, not to belittle or to condemn.

As we hear of problems at Fannie Mae, Lehman Brothers, Bear Stearns, Countrywide Financial, AIG, the "Big Three", and many others, we see the "experts" on TV bandying various strategies that they say will "make the pain go away". Sooner or later someone inevitably throws out some gargantuan dollar amount that they hope will "clean up the mess". But even on an individual level, if someone who is rich and famous can still get hooked on drugs or commit suicide, do politicians really believe that money alone can solve problems at the macro level? (Of course this also ignores the discussion of who will pay for these "capital infusions.") Let me say it as loudly and as clearly as I possibly can: Spiritual Problems CANNOT be solved with financial strategies.

"What spiritual problems," you ask? Let's briefly look at two:

1) God says "You shall have no other gods before me." I believe America has so many gods ahead of the one true God that He might as well be in the back of the line at Baskin-Robbins (you know, take a number?). What gods? How about Food, Sports, Comfort, Entertainment, Beauty, Fitness, Money, Sex, Drugs, or Power? There are many more, though a few of these can be worthy, if put in proper perspective: at times they can be great servants, but they always make poor masters. For more insights, read the 1st and 2nd chapters of Romans, which say it much better than I can.

2) Proverbs 21:5 says that steady plodding brings prosperity, but hasty speculation brings poverty. Many Christians today are as guilty as anyone else of being oblivious to the financial lies that have crept into our society. False gods of greed and consumerism, assumptions that "bigger is always better" and the tyranny of quarterly reports have each led us all too often to join our "unspiritual" neighbors in worshiping at the church of mammon.

There are all kinds of financial "traps" that Satan uses to try to ensnare us. Far too many times we have bought into his lies. We assume, for instance, that progressively greater consumption of goods is always beneficial, that a desire for "things" has more importance than a meaningful philosophy of life, that we should never suffer or have a wrinkle, that we're "entitled" to a long "retirement," and that wealth, not God, is the answer to any and all of our problems.
Many Christians have become as addicted to debt as non-Christians. As long as we serve the gods of this world, it doesn't matter what "quick fixes" or investment solutions we try. I know whereof I speak. In the early 1990's I almost bankrupted my family. We lived on credit cards for almost 4 years, until at one point we owed more on cards than many people owe on their house.

As sure as I am that our problems have spiritual roots, I'm equally sure that there are some, even in the Church, who may question what I'm saying here. I am not a prophet, but people also laughed at Noah until it began to rain and God shut the door on the Ark. I believe it's beginning to rain on our economy. It's OK for you to be skeptical, but where will you look for answers, and how long will you wait before you acknowledge Truth? My advice? Don't wait for the door to shut. . . .

Later in the book of Genesis, God couldn't allow Joseph to be the 2nd most powerful man in Egypt until Joseph's heart was right. The Bible says if we seek God, we will find Him, IF we seek Him with all our heart. I confess that my heart is too often tainted with thinking that is light years away from what God teaches in His Word. So if you disagree with my conclusions, make sure your alternative truly comes from God's recommendations, not from spiritual half-truths.

My hope for this book is that I can bring enough truth to light, so that we will all be inspired to do like Noah in Genesis 6:9 and "walk with God." Far too many Christians have thought we were doing all that is necessary by attending church for one hour per week. What would your health be like if you only ate once a week? Or what if you only exercised one time per week? For some of us, engaging in both of those activities only one time per week might be a temporary improvement! But the long term results would still be calamitous.

Please don't think I'm trying to convey that I am perfect, or that I have all the answers. I have lived for almost 60 years, so what I bring to the table is 40 years as an "adult" who has made far too many mistakes. And I've experienced plenty of heartaches from disobeying God. But God has been faithful to our family, even when I didn't deserve it, so I pray that some of my brokenness will help you avoid the pitfalls that my family and I have survived only by the grace of God.

I challenge you to do whatever you have to do, to read a daily lesson in this book every day for 40 days. Renew your mind and build your heart, so that you can have peace during the storm, because money cannot and will not bring true peace. If we are brave enough[1] and humble enough[2] to admit our failures, God is waiting for us. He longs to restore us and to restore our country.

[1] Matthew 5:3, *"Blessed are the poor in spirit, because the kingdom of heaven is theirs."*

[2] 2 Chronicles 7:14, *"If My people, who are called by My name, shall humble themselves, pray, seek, crave, and require of necessity My face and turn from their wicked ways, then will I hear from heaven, forgive their sin, and heal their land."* (Amp.)

Introduction

The motivation to write a book began as I observed various media personalities giving advice that I felt could have been much more appropriate and personalized. After I had written most of the book, I realized that I really had 2 books. So this first book is my attempt to be "salt and light" to people who are lost, confused, hurting, and/or searching in these uncertain economic times. I hope that you will not only read this book, but that you will also study God's Word and seek His specific *rhema*[1] for you in each of your individual situations. Remember, Jesus didn't heal blind eyes the same way each time.

I know in my own life, I have depended too often on someone to "spoon feed" me. So I hope that what I write here will help all of us to be less dependent on someone else's research, and to walk (closer) with God. This book has 40 main lessons, each of which can be read in less than 5 minutes. Then we included some thought-provoking questions for you to reflect on as you go through each of the 40 days. We also included a daily scripture that you can memorize or meditate on each day. That way you're "marinating" in God's Word, not just speed-reading it. The scriptures were chosen to help prepare your heart for the following day's lesson. As an added bonus, I've included a few extra scriptures and some thoughts related to some of America's better-known holidays.

It is also my hope that non-Christians will be able to profit from most, if not all, of these lessons. There are many principles in this study which have helped people of all faiths to build wealth. If you do not have a Bible and would like to receive one, please let us know. I belong to Gideons International, and if at all possible, I will try to see that you receive a Bible from the Gideons.

May this book help each of you experience God's very best in every area of your life.

Steve Sappington
September 10, 2008

[1] for more information, see http://encyclopedia.thefreedictionary.com/Rhema or http://en.wikipedia.org/wiki/Rhema

- Day 1 -

Today's WORD on Money™: The Most Valuable Thing on Earth

So God tells us that our eternal existence and well-being are FAR more valuable than EVERYTHING material, which is temporary at best.

What if something you thought was true turned out NOT to be true? When would you want to know that it was indeed not true? The goal of Today's WORD on Money™ is to share Biblical wealth principles that you can implement NOW before it's too late. And by the way, if you're still alive, it's never too late to make at least some improvement in your life, perhaps even an eternal improvement.

The Bible has well over 2000 scriptures dealing with money and wealth, so evidently God knows we need lots of help when it comes to managing finances. And He wants us to use money as a tool, not as an idol to worship. Over the next 40 days, we will look at some of the key scriptures which can help us apply Biblical principles to the wealth that God entrusts to us.

Today, let's put first things first: what is the MOST VALUABLE thing on earth? There are literally 100's of scriptures which can help us answer this question, and I encourage you to study beyond what our brief devotionals will cover. Why do I say this? Because God tells us in the Bible that He wants to have a personal relationship with each and every one of us! I know that may be hard for some of you to believe right now, but that's why He created us.

In spite of all of our shortcomings, and in spite of all of the evil that is temporarily on this planet, the King of the Universe truly cares for each and every one of us. He has countless wonderful secrets intended just for you, if you'll only learn to communicate with Him. So don't be like the Hebrews at Mt. Sinai, when they wanted Moses to tell them God's words, instead of hearing God for themselves. (Exodus 20:19, Deuteronomy 5:25-27)

For today, though, so that you don't think that what I'm saying is impossible, or in case Bible study is new to you, let me help you get started. Matthew 16:26 reads, "*And how do you benefit if you gain the whole world but lose your own soul (life) in the process? Is anything worth more than your soul*?" The Message translation reads, "*What kind of deal is it to get everything you want but lose yourself? What could you ever trade your soul for*?"

So God tells us that our eternal existence and well-being are FAR more valuable than EVERYTHING material, which is temporary at best. (Here are just a few of the many additional verses you can study: Jeremiah 29:11, Deuteronomy 8:18, Matthew 5:16, Romans 3:5-6 and 8:31, Hosea 6:3, Matthew 6:33, and Luke 6:38.)

Tomorrow, we'll learn more about who truly owns this most valuable of all assets.

"Paradigm Shifters—Action Points"

1) Make a list of some things you once believed that you now know are not true.

Santa Claus____

____

____

____

____

2) Did someone ever try to change your mind about something, but you weren't ready to receive it? How would your life be different if you had received it sooner? Sometimes we are all too much like the Pharisees were, unwilling and/or unable to see the truth because of our traditions. Is there anything now that you know you need to change? God loves it when we run *to* Him, not *from* Him. As in the story of the Prodigal Son, God welcomes us with open arms.

____

____

____

____

3) In what have you placed too much value or trust? God's Word says we should have no other gods before or above Him. I once heard of a Christian lady from India who said she didn't like to visit America because we have so many idols over here! Ask someone who knows you well if they see something that you've made more important than your relationship with God.

____

____

____

____

____

____

____

____

Day 1 Selah-Meditations

(How would you like to have 40 more scriptures "hidden in your heart"? If so, pick your favorite translation below and memorize it. Watch how God's Word recharges you and how you grow in your walk with Jesus. Even if you don't memorize it, if you meditate on a verse throughout each day, over the next 40 days you will have cultivated a great habit!)

Proverbs 11:30

The fruit of the righteous is a tree of life; and he that winneth souls is wise. (KJV)

The fruit of the righteous is a tree of life, And he who is wise wins souls. (NASB)

A good life is a fruit-bearing tree; a violent life destroys souls. (Message)

The fruit of the [uncompromisingly] righteous is a tree of life, and he who is wise captures human lives [for God, as a fisher of men--he gathers and receives them for eternity]. (Amplified)

The seeds of good deeds become a tree of life; a wise person wins friends. (NLT)

The fruit of the righteous is a tree of life, but violence takes lives. (HCSB)

- Day 2 -

Today's WORD on Money™:

Who Owns It?

If you are serious about finding out what your own stewardship responsibilities are, a good place to begin is by studying the Parable of the Talents . . . .

So far, we have learned that each of us has an eternal soul that is worth more than every material possession on earth: not just any possession—every possession! So who owns all of these assets?

Psalm 24:1 says "*The earth is the Lord's and everything in it. The world and all its people belong to God*[1]." On the other hand, Psalm 115:16 says "*The heavens are the LORD's, but the earth He has given to the human race*." (HCSB)[2] After reading these and other passages, some people may conclude that God made everything and then only expects 10% back from us. Others will conclude that God still owns 100% and that we are to be stewards. But even those who emphasize personal ownership of the 90% will generally agree that we need to commit and dedicate everything to God, so that no enemy can invade what God has given us. Whether we see ourselves as stewards or as owners, for the purposes of this book our focus will be that all followers of Christ should manage all that's entrusted to us according to God's will, so that His "kingdom comes" and His will is "done, on earth as it is in Heaven." Thus I believe we can all agree that God expects us to be good, wise, profitable managers (Matthew 10:16 and 25: 14-30). Further, I believe that we can gain much wisdom by examining the traits of all four of the major characters in the Parable of the Talents. While I prefer to write in terms of stewardship, if you prefer to replace my "stewardship" terminology with "owner" or "manager" language, be my guest.

So how are we expected to manage the assets God entrusts to each of us? If you are serious about finding out what your own stewardship responsibilities are, a good place to begin is by studying the Parable of the Talents, found in Matthew 25:14-30 and in Luke 19:12-27. This story contains more than a dozen economic and wealth stewardship principles[3]. We will cover some of these principles in our future lessons.

By contrast, in Luke 15 we see an example of what not to do, as we read the Parable of the Prodigal Son (Luke 15:11-32). One lesson from this parable is that we can waste and even lose our gifts if we ignore or reject God's instructions for how to succeed in life.

Various Bible passages[4] teach us that we should be diligent, and that we are to view work as one of the many ways in which we should gratefully worship God, the giver of all good gifts. We also learn that God actually expects us to be profitable[5].

For those of you who feel called to the workplace, especially those who already own or want to own your own business, we encourage you to take courses in Biblical Entrepreneurship. (See the footnotes below, or our website for more details.) Tomorrow, we'll look at some ways to apply what we've learned about what God says is His most valuable asset.

[1] See also Deuteronomy 28, 32:65, Psalm 71, 100 and 139, Haggai 2:8, Colossians 3:10, Ephesians 2:10 and 3:9

[2] See also Psalm 50:10-12

[3] Biblical Entrepreneurship was developed by Patrice Tsague, www.nehemiahproject.org.

[4] Psalm 119:98-99, Proverbs 13:22, Micah 6:8, Luke 11:9-13, Mark 12:29-31, John 12:20-26, John 13:34, Ephesians 2:14, Colossians 1:10 and 3:17, 23.

[5] See also books like God at Work by David W. Miller, God Is at Work by Ken Eldred, God @ Work by Rich Marshall, and The Elk River Story by Rick Heeren.

See also Psalm 50:10-12

"Paradigm Shifters—Action Points"

1) Study the parable of the talents and see if you can find at least 12 economic principles there. Which principles play to your strengths? How about your weaknesses? Ask God how He would have you use this passage to improve your stewardship.

____

____

____

____

2) Seek out someone you know who might be willing to mentor you or disciple you, so that you can more fully "*walk in all of the good works which God prepared for you*." (Ephesians 2:10)

____

____

____

____

3) Be ready and willing to mentor someone else, even if it's only for a moment, speaking an encouraging observation to them. Ask God to help you discover whom He wants you to mentor, and for how long. (2 Timothy 2:2)

____

____

____

____

Day 2 Selah-Meditations

Philemon v. 6

That the communication of thy faith may become effectual by the acknowledging of every good thing which is in you in Christ Jesus. (KJV)

[And I pray] that the participation in and sharing of your faith may produce and promote full recognition and appreciation and understanding and precise knowledge of every good [thing] that is ours in [our identification with] Christ Jesus [and unto His glory]. (Amplified)

And I am praying that you will put into action the generosity that comes from your faith as you understand and experience all the good things we have in Christ. (NLT)

that the fellowship of thy faith may become effectual, in the knowledge of every good thing which is in you, unto Christ. (ASV)

that the fellowship of thy faith may become working in the full knowledge of every good thing that [is] in you toward Christ Jesus; (YLT)

I pray that you will be active in sharing what you believe. Then you will completely understand every good thing we have in Christ. (New International Reader's Version)

I pray that you may be active in sharing your faith, so that you will have a full understanding of every good thing we have in Christ. (NIV)

and I pray that the fellowship of your faith may become effective through the knowledge of every good thing which is in you for Christ's sake. (NASB)

And I keep praying that this faith we hold in common keeps showing up in the good things we do, and that people recognize Christ in all of it. (Message)

[I pray] that your participation in the faith may become effective through knowing every good thing that is in us for [the glory of] Christ. (HCSB)

in such sort that thy participation in the faith should become operative in the acknowledgment of every good thing which is in us towards Christ [Jesus]. (Darby)

That the sharing of your faith may become effective by the acknowledgement of every good thing that is in you in Christ Jesus (the Anointed Savior Who lives in you, and you in Him, and because of His Anointing on you). (Steve's multi-translation compilation!)

Day 3

Today's WORD on Money™: The Best Investment You Can Make Now

Even though Christians should not gamble or rely on games of chance, it does not follow that we should never make financial investments.

Yesterday we examined the issue of ownership. The Bible also teaches that God gives us the freedom to accept or reject His authority in our lives. But before proceeding any further, let's answer the question I'm most frequently asked: "Where is the best place to invest now?"

Earlier, we learned that each person's eternal soul is worth more than everything on earth (Matthew 16:26). Things are temporary but souls are eternal. In Matthew 13, Jesus tells about a sower who harvests 100 times as much as he planted. In financial terms, that would be like investing $1000 and turning it into $100,000!

Most people think that gambling, not investing, is the only activity that might bring them a hundred-to-one return. Yet the Bible tells us that, instead of relying on "luck," which really doesn't even exist, anyone who follows God's system has the potential to receive a 100-fold return. In other words, God wants all of his children to win, not just one person. So the Bible teaches that only blessings and cursings exist, not good luck and bad luck.

Soon, we'll cover more on the topic of how to be blessed and not cursed. But in terms of investing, even a brief study of scripture reveals that if we help even one person change his or her eternal destination, we will receive a higher, spiritual return than that very rare person who receives a 100-to-1 monetary return.

Even though Christians should not gamble or rely on games of chance, it does not follow that we should never make financial investments. In fact, Matthew 25:27 teaches that good stewardship requires that we make a profit. Sometimes God may direct us to grow and hold assets for a period of time. But we must remember that the time may come when God asks us to use earthly profits to harvest heavenly treasure. I don't know about you, but I frequently need to remind myself that God is my source, and not any of the assets that God entrusts to me for a season.

Some of our studies will mention ways to increase our financial profitability, because we are expected to make a monetary profit. But let us never lose sight of the fact that investing in God's Kingdom is ultimately THE most profitable investment we can make.

"Paradigm Shifters—Action Points"

1) What can you do that will help you "Practice the Presence" of God, so that you're more aware of opportunities to "get a better (eternal) return"?

____

____

____

____

____

____

____

____

2) Have you ever acknowledged God's ownership of everything in your life? If not, what is holding you back and what are you holding back? In future lessons, we will discuss how faith levels can be related to your love for God.

____

____

____

____

____

____

____

____

Day 3 Selah-Meditations

2 Timothy 2:15

Study to shew thyself approved unto God, a workman that needeth not to be ashamed, rightly dividing the word of truth. (KJV)

Be diligent to present yourself approved to God as a workman who does not need to be ashamed, accurately handling the word of truth. (NASB)

Concentrate on doing your best for God, work you won't be ashamed of, laying out the truth plain and simple. (Message)

Study and be eager and do your utmost to present yourself to God approved (tested by trial), a workman who has no cause to be ashamed, correctly analyzing and accurately dividing [rightly handling and skillfully teaching] the Word of Truth. (Amplified)

Work hard so you can present yourself to God and receive his approval. Be a good worker, one who does not need to be ashamed and who correctly explains the word of truth. (NLT)

be diligent to present thyself approved to God -- a workman irreproachable, rightly dividing the word of the truth; (YLT)

Be diligent to present yourself approved to God, a worker who doesn't need to be ashamed, correctly teaching the word of truth. (HCSB)

Strive diligently to present thyself approved to God, a workman that has not to be ashamed, cutting in a straight line the word of truth. (Darby)

Busily keep [Busily care, *or keep,*] to give thyself an approved, praiseable workman to God, without shame, rightly treating the word of truth. (Wycliffe NT)

- Day 4 -

Today's WORD on Money™: Provision for Risk

For an excellent study of a warrior in the Bible who had to deal with risk, look no further than King David.

How do you protect yourself against risk? Today we'll look at a few kinds of risk, and how we can make provision.

Only God can truly protect us from risk. But as good stewards, we should not "tempt God." (Matthew 4:7) One reason I recommend whole life insurance for some clients is that it can be part of an overall strategy to pay off debt. For example, as the cash value builds up in a policy, the "owner" can begin to self-insure for smaller risks by increasing the deductibles on policies which insure property and assets. As you increase these deductibles, "P&C"[1] policy premiums can decrease, which frees up funds that can build more cash value in a life insurance policy; increased cash value can then be used to purchase assets with money that you control and pay back to yourself, instead of paying someone else. In other words, clients can build their own self-financing systems. This process can have a multiplier effect on the assets a person stewards. So for the right company or individual, so-called "permanent" insurance can be a way to increase stewardship by multiplying "talents[2]."

As a recent example of risk, September 11, 2001 vividly reminds us how quickly life can change. I also work with clients who serve as missionaries around the world. In addition, there are numerous wars being fought at any given time. As good stewards, we need to be prudent. My friend Frank Reynolds says that we should "work hard like it depends on us, but pray hard because we know it depends on God." I believe this principle also applies to risk management.

On the spiritual level, which affects all other areas of life, our family pleads the blood of Jesus over our lives, and over everything we say, think, do, have, and everywhere we go. And we also do what we believe God would have us do in terms of having adequate insurance to replace the things we use in our daily lives. We don't say that the insurance companies protect us. But we can transfer risk to these companies, while knowing that ultimately only God can protect us.

For an excellent study of a warrior in the Bible who had to deal with risk, look no further than King David. Shortly after killing Goliath, he lived for many years either on the run or face to face with King Saul, who must have been manic-depressive. Craig Fryar is an Austin businessman who works with venture capital. He spoke to our Integrate Business[3] luncheon in 2007 and showed us a verse that I have since memorized--Psalm 143:8. It says "Let the morning bring me word of Your unfailing love, for I have put my trust in You. Show me the way I should go, for to You I lift up my soul." If we don't read the rest of Psalm 143 or know more about David's life, we may not appreciate these words. But David went through many tough, lonely times.

In America, there are many who have risked their lives so that we can enjoy a life filled with freedoms. I encourage you to cultivate an attitude of thanks for these freedoms. And I speak blessings of peace, safety, and wholeness on you and your families. In the Old Testament, the Hebrew sometimes says "shalom shalom," which as I understand it, means more than "peace, peace." It means "perfect peace," with "nothing missing, nothing broken." So may you and your loved ones know shalom shalom.

[1] Property and Casualty

[2] Our website has more information on this topic.

[3] http://www.antiochcc.net

"Paradigm Shifters--Action Points"

1) Please remember what we covered in our first lesson: "What if something you thought was true turned out NOT to be true? When would you want to know that it was indeed not true?" If I read scriptures right, Jesus didn't just say that the Truth would set us free. It's only the Truth that we know that sets us free. Not knowing the truth can be extremely risky.

____

____

____

2) Here's another observation about truth and risk in a different arena: isn't it interesting that in many circles, it's more important to be "tolerant" than it is to know the truth? Since so many people have not realized the implausibility of theories like evolution, they allow themselves to be fooled into thinking that all paths lead to Heaven. If this were true, then Jesus' suffering and death on the cross were unnecessary. I saw Oprah on YouTube[4], asking a hypothetical question about someone who grew up and never heard about Jesus, but who lived "as Jesus would have had you to live." She evidently believed that such a person would go to Heaven. But her theory, while "rational," is flawed, because she hasn't studied scripture. Romans 3:23 clearly says that "all have sinned and fall short of the glory of God." So her imaginary person who "lived with a loving heart" does not exist in reality. Now before we get "holier than thou" and start "pointing fingers" at Oprah, let's thank God that she has a heart to serve and that she has tried to help millions of people. Because of that, we should pray for her to be blessed: someone who is truly blessed knows the truth and can experience God's best in every area of life. So let's pray that all of us, including Oprah, minimize temporal and eternal risk by knowing the way, the Truth, the life, the peace, and the salvation of God[5].

____

____

____

____

3) Ann Coulter's book Godless has a multi-chapter refutation of evolution. Ben Stein's movie Expelled also confronts those who supposedly believe in the scientific questioning process. Isn't it interesting that those who believe in evolution or in "tolerance" are so often intolerant of other viewpoints? They evidently are so threatened that they try to suppress other perspectives. Islam must also have such doubts about its own veracity, since it can't "tolerate" someone who converts to Christianity. Many converts in Muslim countries have lost their families, and even their lives, when they asked Jesus to be their Lord and Savior. My hero in the "tolerance department" is Elijah. In 1 Kings 18:24, he said, "And you call on the name of your god, and I will call on the name of the LORD, and the God who answers by fire, He is God." I think Christians need to do more of this today. Of course, that means that we'd better be "prayed up" and ready to deal with the enemy's attacks.

I tell evolutionists that they have more faith than I do! In light of the 2nd Law of Thermodynamics (e.g., the quality of matter/energy deteriorates gradually over time) and Mendel's studies in genetics (seeds "break down" over generations), it takes an enormous amount of "blind faith" to believe that "things" defy proven laws and grow more complex through a theoretical process called evolution.

[4] http://www.youtube.com/watch?v=F-HNNAqJrxw

[5] *"For the wages of sin is death; but the gift of God is eternal life through Christ Jesus our Lord."* (Romans 6:23 KJV)

Day 4 Selah-Meditations

(I heard one pastor say that this verse inspired him to get a name plate for his desk with the one word "Always" inscribed on it!)

2 Corinthians 2:14

Now thanks be unto God, which always causeth us to triumph in Christ, and maketh manifest the savour of his knowledge by us in every place. (KJV)

But thanks be to God, who always leads us in triumph in Christ, and manifests through us the sweet aroma of the knowledge of Him in every place. (NASB)

And I got it, thank God! In the Messiah, in Christ, God leads us from place to place in one perpetual victory parade. Through us, he brings knowledge of Christ. Everywhere we go, people breathe in the exquisite fragrance. (Message)

But thanks be to God, Who in Christ always leads us in triumph [as trophies of Christ's victory] and through us spreads and makes evident the fragrance of the knowledge of God everywhere, (Amplified)

But thank God! He has made us his captives and continues to lead us along in Christ's triumphal procession. Now he uses us to spread the knowledge of Christ everywhere, like a sweet perfume. (NLT)

and to God [are] thanks, who at all times is leading us in triumph in the Christ, and the fragrance of His knowledge He is manifesting through us in every place, (YLT)

But thanks be to God, who always puts us on display in Christ, and spreads through us in every place the scent of knowing Him. (HCSB)

But thanks [be] to God, who always leads us in triumph in the Christ, and makes manifest the odour of his knowledge through us in every place. (Darby)

And I do thankings to God, that evermore maketh us to have victory in Christ Jesus, and showeth by us the odour of his knowing in each place; (Wycliffe NT)

- Day 5 -

Today's WORD on Money™: How Much Should You Keep in Your Accounts?

But how often do many Christians say that God owns everything, and then half an hour later, we get into "our" cars, drive to "our" homes, and look up the balances in "our" accounts before we give "our" money to help someone in need?!

How much money should you keep in your savings account? How about your IRA's, your CD's, your real estate or your other investments? Actually the number should be ZERO.

Yesterday we learned that the most profitable investment we can make is to invest in God's Kingdom and in what He values. A return that benefits someone for eternity far surpasses a return of 100-to-1, or even a thousand-to-one, or more. But we also learned that God wants us to be profitable in every aspect of our daily lives, so there are times when we should make financial investments. In fact, we will soon examine how wise financial stewardship is necessary to equip us for reaping spiritual or Kingdom harvests (1 Tim. 6:18).

So then isn't it a mistake for me to tell you to keep a ZERO balance in your savings and investment accounts? Not at all. Remember, on Day 2 we learned that everything we have comes from God[1]. We are stewards, called to make a profit for our Maker, and someday we will be required to "render an account" to God of all that we were given to manage. Martin Luther said, "I should say that security is the greatest of all idols." So if we place our trust in "stuff," rather than committing everything to God, ownership becomes a curse.

We become more vulnerable to attacks from the enemy, and more likely to waste or lose what God has given us. In my life, I have found that I'm actually more "prosperous" when I look for ways to become a better steward and to manage things for God's purposes rather than for my own selfish reasons.

So my point is not that your accounts should be empty[2], but that they should be committed and dedicated to God! Again, let me re-emphasize: we are to be good stewards. We must take seriously the management of what God entrusts to us. I can hear some of you saying, "Come on, Steve, that was a trick question." Perhaps. But how often do many Christians say that God owns everything, and then half an hour later, we get into "our" cars, drive to "our" homes, and look up the balances in "our" accounts before we give "our" money to help someone in need?! If we treat everything as "ours" without committing and dedicating it to God, it is subject to being killed, stolen or destroyed.[3] If you are like me and have sometimes been ungrateful or negligent in asking for God's protection, you may even want to renew your words regarding the accounts you manage. For example, you might try saying "this" account or "God's" account, or even "Blessing #123," instead of saying "my" account.

Tomorrow we'll talk about retirement accounts.

[1] Remember Deuteronomy 8:18 also: even our ability to get wealth comes from God.

[2] I'm sorry to disappoint any of you who thought you were in God's will by having empty accounts!

[3] John 10:10

"Paradigm Shifters—Action Points"

1) Make a list of at least 3 things that you sometimes forget to commit and dedicate to God. Which one will you focus on, until you develop the habit of being a better steward?

____

____

____

____

2) Ask God to show you any "talent" that you've buried. It could be "false humility," such as being overly modest when receiving repeated compliments. What gifts did God give you in order to bless His other children, who are your sisters and brothers? What gifts do you have that could bring someone to God, someone who might not meet anyone else who can reach them like you can? For example, I know that two of my gifts are teaching and writing. Writing this book enables me to increase the number of potential "students" that I can reach.

____

____

____

____

3) Have you taken credit for a talent or skill, rather than acknowledging it as God's gift to you? (Even a bent toward hard work is not really something we can take much credit for.)

____

____

____

____

____

____

4) I heard comedian Steve Harvey say that he had a passion for basketball, but it wasn't his gift. His gift is comedy. Your gift is what you do best with the least amount of effort. What's your gift? How does God want you to use it? Find out, and Psalm 37:4 will manifest in your life: "Delight yourself also in the Lord, and He shall give you the desires of your heart."

____

____

____

____

____

____

Day 5 Selah-Meditations

Matthew 5:16

Let your light so shine before men, that they may see your good works, and glorify your Father which is in heaven. (KJV)

Let your light shine before men in such a way that they may see your good works, and glorify your Father who is in heaven. (NASB)

Now that I've put you there on a hilltop, on a light stand—shine! Keep open house; be generous with your lives. By opening up to others, you'll prompt people to open up with God, this generous Father in heaven. (Message)

Let your light so shine before men that they may see your moral excellence and your praiseworthy, noble, and good deeds and recognize and honor and praise and glorify your Father Who is in heaven. (Amplified)

In the same way, let your good deeds shine out for all to see, so that everyone will praise your heavenly Father. (NLT)

so let your light shine before men, that they may see your good works, and may glorify your Father who [is] in the heavens. (YLT)

In the same way, let your light shine before men, so that they may see your good works and give glory to your Father in heaven. (HCSB)

Let your light thus shine before men, so that they may see your upright works, and glorify your Father who is in the heavens. (Darby)

So shine your light before men, that they see your good works, and glorify your Father that is in heavens. (Wycliffe NT)

- Day 6 -

Today's WORD on Money™: What Does the Bible Say About Retirement?

But my point is this: whether or not we continue to work or to be employed in the workplace, we are all called first and foremost to be about God's business.

Did you know that "retirement" is a fairly recent concept? What does the Bible say about when we should retire[1]?

As I've studied scripture, about the only instructions I can find concerning retirement are in Numbers 8:24-25 when the Lord told Moses that the Levites at age 50 should retire from performing some of their duties in the Tabernacle. Other than that, it appears that we are to be like the Apostle Paul and continue to "run the race" as long as we're here on earth. I'm sure most of us know of someone who has continued to witness for God even on his or her death bed. Moses himself kept working until the day he died at age 120. And the Bible says that when he died, Moses' "*eye was not dim, nor his natural force abated.*" (Deuteronomy 34:7) That should tell us something about one of the many benefits of a personal relationship with God[2]!

So does that mean we're to have a physical job as long as we're alive? Not necessarily, although I've seen many senior adults who are better workers than some people who are in their 20's and 30's. But my point is this: whether or not we continue to work or to be employed in the workplace, we are all called first and foremost to be about God's business. Matthew 28:19-20 (called "The Great Commission" by many) says this, "*Go ye therefore, and teach all nations, baptizing them in the name of the Father, and of the Son, and of the Holy Spirit: Teaching them to observe all things whatsoever I have commanded you: and, lo, I am with you always, even unto the end of the world.*"

So then, as Matthew 5:16 says, we're to let the light of God shine through us, so that people see good works that lead them to glorify God. So does that mean we should all quit our jobs and become missionaries? We'll examine that question next.

[1] To learn more about these "outside-the-box, inside-the-Kingdom" concepts, see our website, or turn to the back page of this book, which was taken from our site. If you are an advisor who would like to know more about teaching Biblical financial concepts to churches, ministries, and donors, please contact us for more information.

Also, please contact us if the concept of Biblical Entrepreneurship appeals to you. We can help you learn about when and where classes are offered. Or you can visit www.nehemiahproject.org (Patrice Tsague).

[2] Refer to our Day 1 discussion on learning to communicate with God.

"Paradigm Shifters—Action Points"

1) Study how the concept of "retirement" was influenced by Bismarck in Germany in the late 1800's, and then by FDR in the 1930's. Has "retirement" affected how senior adults view themselves? Has it affected how they are viewed by young people? What can you do to change these stereotypes and walk in Christian love?

____

____

____

____

2) Have you developed a plan to be able to "redirect" if God leads you to do so? Will what you do provide an income, like the Apostle Paul ("tentmaker")? Or will you need to save money now to be used later? If so, how much? If you don't have the requisite software and planning skills, you'll want to get help from a financial professional to calculate what your numbers should be. Why not give yourself a deadline to have a plan completed? Watch how the plan energizes and focuses your daily actions.

____

____

____

____

3) What opportunities do you have right now to "let your light shine"?

____

____

____

____

Day 6 Selah-Meditations

Psalm 37:4

Delight thyself also in the LORD: and he shall give thee the desires of thine heart. (KJV)

Delight yourself in the LORD; And He will give you the desires of your heart. (NASB)

Keep company with God, get in on the best. (Message)

Delight yourself also in the Lord, and He will give you the desires and secret petitions of your heart. (Amplified)

Take delight in the Lord, and he will give you your heart's desires. (NLT)

And delight thyself on Jehovah, And He giveth to thee the petitions of thy heart. (YLT)

Take delight in the LORD, and He will give you your heart's desires. (HCSB)

and delight thyself in Jehovah, and he will give thee the desires of thy heart. (Darby)

- Day 7 -

Today's WORD on Money™:

Are You Supposed to be in Business or in Ministry?

So really, all Christians should be "in the ministry" no matter what our occupation is.

Most people have to spend at least part of their lives working in order to have enough money to support themselves. (Gen. 3:19; 1 Tim. 5:8, 18) Many Christians struggle with how much money is enough, and with whether or not they should go into "full-time ministry." So what does the Bible say about who is supposed to be "in the ministry"?

In the 21st Century, most of us with a "Western" mindset make a distinction between things that are "sacred" and things that are "secular." But if we study both the Old and New Testaments, we learn that the Jews rarely, if ever, made such a distinction. Everything they did was to be "as unto the Lord." (Eccl. 9:10; Eph. 5:20; Col. 1:12, 3:17, 23; 1 Cor. 10:31; 1 Thess. 4:10-11; 2 Thess. 3:13; 1 Tim. 6: 17-19; 2 Tim. 2:15)

So really, all Christians should be "in the ministry" no matter what our occupation is. In our last lesson, we learned how the Bible teaches that we are to be "salt and light" to the surrounding world. That means that in whatever career God directs us to pursue, our overriding purpose should be to value the 3 things God values: salvation, discipleship, and service. Then as we minister and honor God in our daily lives, He promises that He will draw people up into a relationship with Him (John 12:32).

Since many people do not currently attend church, they will never see all that God has to offer them if we don't let them see Jesus in us wherever we are, 7 days a week. (2 Cor. 2:14) When we begin to take this aspect of ministry more seriously, then we will encounter fewer people in America who know as little about Jesus as those who live in far more remote areas of the world. We'll also hear less about Christian "hypocrites" whose actions have lead others away from Jesus (the Way, the Truth, and the Life, John 14:6).

Jesus said He was to be about His Father's business (Luke 2:49), and Ephesians says we are to be imitators of God (Ephesians 5:1). I can't think of a better way to thank God for all He's done for us than to do all we can to be in daily, "full-time" ministry, taking back God's territory from Satan and his fellow trespassers (Matthew 11:12).

So the next time someone asks you what you do for a living, why not tell them that you're in "full time ministry"?! Who knows, that may open the door for you to tell them how much God loves them, how He wants to minister to us all, and how He wants all of His children to be "in the ministry." (3 John 2, Jeremiah 29:11, John 10:10) In our future lessons, we'll examine ways that people can see a difference in us by the way we handle money. Tomorrow we'll look at how our spiritual convictions can affect how we save money for the future.

"Paradigm Shifters—Action Points"

1) Examine your daily routines. Should you conduct more activities "as unto the Lord"? When I used to counsel people who had been spending too much, one recommendation I usually made was for them to keep a spending log for at least a month, writing down every purchase they made. You can use that same strategy to become aware of ways you can live that are more focused on letting your light shine. Write down with whom you meet and interact, and reflect on what you said and did to let them see Jesus in your life. Then ask God to show you how to improve. Guess what? He will!

____

____

____

2) 1 John 2:16 talks about the "lust of the flesh." The Amplified translation says it this way: "*For all that is in the world--the lust of the flesh [craving for sensual gratification] and the lust of the eyes [greedy longings of the mind] and the pride of life [assurance in one's own resources or in the stability of earthly things]--these do not come from the Father but are from the world [itself].*" Recent economic events reveal the end results of lust, greed, and pride. I think you'll find that almost all financial problems stem from one or more of these three ways that people try to meet needs that only God can meet.

____

____

____

____

3) At age 85, Caleb said "Give me that mountain." Caleb is one of my heroes. He was as strong at age 85 as he had been 40 years earlier. What mountains does God still want <u>you</u> to conquer?

Day 7 Selah-Meditations

(Notice in the Amplified version, that the inheritance is not just financial.)

Proverbs 13:22

A good man leaveth an inheritance to his children's children: and the wealth of the sinner is laid up for the just. (KJV)

A good man leaves an inheritance to his children's children, And the wealth of the sinner is stored up for the righteous. (NASB)

A good life gets passed on to the grandchildren; ill-gotten wealth ends up with good people. (Message)

A good man leaves an inheritance [of moral stability and goodness] to his children's children, and the wealth of the sinner [finds its way eventually] into the hands of the righteous, for whom it was laid up. (Amplified)

Good people leave an inheritance to their grandchildren, but the sinner's wealth passes to the godly. (NLT)

A good man causeth sons' sons to inherit, And laid up for the righteous [is] the sinner's wealth. (YLT)

A good man leaves an inheritance to his grandchildren, but the sinner's wealth is stored up for the righteous. (HCSB)

A good man leaveth an inheritance to his children's children; but the wealth of the sinner is laid up for the righteous [man]. (Darby)

- Day 8 -

Today's WORD on Money™:
Little Known Dangers of Retirement Accounts

. . . you should make a retirement account your primary savings vehicle only if you truly believe that your taxes will be substantially lower in 20 years. . . . Placing money in a retirement account delays both the tax AND *the tax calculation.*

As we recently learned, the Bible says almost nothing about retirement. But there are additional reasons why I sometimes think that all literature dealing with Retirement Accounts should have a big red warning label on the front that says, "WARNING!! Retirement Accounts may be hazardous to your wealth!"

If Jesus doesn't return for a while longer, do you think your taxes will be lower or higher 20 years from now? History tells us that, despite what government leaders say, our tax rates will almost certainly be higher. Thus, we believe that you should make a retirement account your primary savings vehicle only if you truly believe that your taxes will be substantially lower in 20 years.

Here's why. Let's assume you save $10,000 in your retirement accounts this year. Let's also assume that your employer matches 50% of everything you contribute. Let's further assume that you're 55 and that you can comfortably retire at age 60. (All of these assumptions are optimistic!) If your tax rate is 33%, and you withdraw that $15,000 ($10,000 contributed by you, $5000 from your employer) from your retirement account, then after taxes, you're back to your original $10,000 contribution! So basically your employer's contribution did not give you a 50% return, it just paid your taxes for you! Now all you have to do is hope that your investment choices outpace inflation, currency fluctuation, accounting irregularities, sub-prime mortgage scandals, credit upheavals and various other risks. If you can do all that, you won't get ahead, but at least you'll break even!

For many people, that whole process is far too complicated. They would be better off and have far less stress, by simply putting money into something tax free, instead of something tax deferred. Tax deferral only delays taxes, it rarely saves you taxes. So you have to ask yourself which risk is greater over the coming 20-30 years: the risk that the stock markets will not perform well, or the risk that your taxes will increase? Until many people have this conversation with us, they are usually under the false impression that market risk should be their main concern.

Here's something else that few people realize: if your investment return and your tax bracket are static for a given period of time, then at the end of that time, after-tax money that grows tax-deferred and comes out tax-free grows to the exact same amount as pre-tax money that grows tax-deferred but is taxed when it comes out! Let us know if you'd like to see an example.

I've often tricked accountants by asking them how much in taxes their client saved by contributing to a retirement account. Rather than a dollar amount, the correct answer is "I don't know. They may not have 'saved' anything. They may have even increased their tax liability. It depends on what the tax rate is when the clients withdraw the money. Placing money in a retirement account delays both the tax AND the tax calculation." We'll examine various tax-advantaged strategies in our next book.

"Paradigm Shifters—Action Points"

1) In one of the seminars that we present to churches and ministries, we share how retirement accounts can be one of many ways to increase donors' ability to give to their children AND to their favorite ministry. We also point out that everyone with a taxable estate will make a charitable donation: they will either donate to whom they want, or they will donate to the IRS. Have you taken adequate steps to ensure that your "donations" will go where you choose for them to go?

____

____

____

____

2) We encourage clients to set "giving goals," just like they set income goals or goals for net worth. Just make sure your goals are what God would have you do, and not what your pride or your ego "thinks" <u>you</u> can do. Why not take some time this weekend to get quiet before the Lord and ask Him what and where He would like you to give?

____

____

____

____

____

____

____

____

Day 8 Selah-Meditations

Proverbs 22:4

By humility and the fear of the LORD are riches, and honour, and life. (KJV)

The reward of humility and the fear of the LORD are riches, honor and life. (NASB)

The payoff for meekness and Fear-of-God is plenty and honor and a satisfying life. (Message)

The reward of humility and the reverent and worshipful fear of the Lord is riches and honor and life. (Amplified)

True humility and fear of the Lord lead to riches, honor, and long life. (NLT)

The end of humility [is] the fear of Jehovah, riches, and honour, and life. (YLT)

The result of humility is fear of the LORD, along with wealth, honor, and life. (HCSB)

The reward of humility [and] the fear of Jehovah is riches, and honour, and life. (Darby)

- Day 9 -

Today's WORD on Money™:
The First Characteristic of an Ideal Investment

. . . if all other variables are equal, then tax-deferred growth and tax-free withdrawal are two very desirable components of an ideal place to save money.

Now that we've learned a few basic Biblical investment concepts, let's spend some time studying investment characteristics. So what do we look for in an ideal place to save money?

First, do you remember why Joseph and Mary were in Bethlehem when Jesus was born? Luke chapter 2 tells us that it was because Caesar Augustus decreed that "all the world" should be taxed. To comply with this decree, Joseph and Mary had to travel to Bethlehem, the home town of Joseph's ancestor David. We can also read about taxes throughout the Old Testament, from Moses, to Solomon, to Xerxes, who ruled from India to Ethiopia. So taxes existed long before the IRS!

We actually know of at least one instance in the New Testament where Jesus paid taxes. In Matthew 17, He had Peter pay their temple tax with a coin found in a fish's mouth (Matthew 17:27). But in 3 of the 4 Gospel accounts, Jesus also taught that it wasn't necessary to pay more taxes than the government requires (Matthew 22:21, Mark 12:17, Luke 20:22-25). These passages also teach that we are to give to God what belongs to God.

So tax advantages are one of the first characteristics many of us desire when considering a place to save money. At this point, we should explain the difference between something tax-deferred and something that is tax-free. Tax deferral simply postpones or delays a tax. The tax must still be paid at some point in the future. On the other hand, a taxpayer can conceivably never have to pay tax on an investment that is tax-free. Some types of investments, entities or strategies can even be tax-free to beneficiaries or to future generations. Thus, one characteristic of an ideal place to save money would be rapid or consistent tax-deferred growth. Then, ideally, we would want the money to be tax-free upon liquidation, at maturity, or even upon inheritance.

To illustrate the benefits of avoiding taxes, let's consider this example. If you were to start with a dollar and double it every day, by Day 20 that dollar would have grown to over $1,000,000! However, if 17% is deducted from each day's growth, that same dollar would grow to less than $178,000! Deducting 27% of each day's growth would result in less than $58,000 by Day 20! For those of you who may be new to investing, let me assure you that there is a big difference between $1,000,000 and $58,000. . . !

However, as we previously discussed, tax deferral may not always be in your best interest, if, for example, tax rates increase over time. But if all other variables are equal, then tax-deferred growth and tax-free withdrawal are two very desirable components of an ideal place to save money. To learn more about investment characteristics, join us as we study our next lesson.

"Paradigm Shifters—Action Points"

1) One of the ways we serve clients is to "help them find money they didn't know they had." Have you met with a financial consultant who knows how to locate money that you are losing unknowingly or unnecessarily? This "transferred wealth" can have a far greater impact on your net worth than merely finding one investment that earns an extra few percentage points. Why not share your financial numbers with someone who knows how to help you "find money"?!

____

____

____

____

2) Ask yourself these questions:

- Is there a better way to pay my mortgage?
- How about my vehicles—am I recapturing the money I spend to purchase them[1]?
- Am I funding my "redirection[2]" funds in the right amounts and in the right ways?
- What is the best way to help my children with education expenses?

These questions will usually produce better answers when you consult with others much like the Bible advises us to do in Proverbs 11:14 and 24:6.

____

____

____

____

[1] See www.infinitebanking.org, and future comments in this book

[2] Or "retirement"

Day 9 Selah-Meditations

(Isn't it amazing to think that even before time began, God knew us and had a purpose for us to accomplish during our time on earth! I know I've often missed His will, but it inspires me and helps me get back on track to know that He has a plan for me, and all I have to do is tap into it!)

Ephesians 2:10

For we are his workmanship, created in Christ Jesus unto good works, which God hath before ordained that we should walk in them. (KJV)

For we are His workmanship, created in Christ Jesus for good works, which God prepared beforehand so that we would walk in them. (NASB)

He creates each of us by Christ Jesus to join him in the work he does, the good work he has gotten ready for us to do, work we had better be doing. (Message)

For we are God's [own] handiwork (His workmanship), recreated in Christ Jesus, [born anew] that we may do those good works which God predestined (planned beforehand) for us [taking paths which He prepared ahead of time], that we should walk in them [living the good life which He prearranged and made ready for us to live]. (Amplified)

For we are God's masterpiece. He has created us anew in Christ Jesus, so we can do the good things he planned for us long ago. (NLT)

for of Him we are workmanship, created in Christ Jesus to good works, which God did before prepare, that in them we may walk. (YLT)

For we are His creation—created in Christ Jesus for good works, which God prepared ahead of time so that we should walk in them. (HCSB)

For we are his workmanship, having been created in Christ Jesus for good works, which God has before prepared that we should walk in them. (Darby)

For we be the making of him, made of nought in Christ Jesus, in good works, which God hath ordained, that we go in those *works* [that God made ready before, that in them we go]. (Wycliffe NT)

- Day 10 -

Today's WORD on Money™:

Risk and Reward

. . . above all, as the Psalmist says, make sure that it's the Lord building your investment "house." Otherwise, your labor will be in vain (Psalm 127:1).

Have you ever heard the phrase "more risk, more reward"? Today we'll learn more about what that phrase means.

I've often joked that most clients want a government-guaranteed account that pays a guaranteed rate of 20+% for life, tax-free, with no penalty for early withdrawal! Of course, no such account exists, but it does highlight some more of the characteristics that we desire in an ideal investment.

If you're driving while you're listening to our program, wait until you're parked to do this. But if you're free to write now, get a piece of paper and write the following 3 investment characteristics from top to bottom:

SAFETY
LIQUIDITY
HIGH RETURN

Here's the rub: almost no single investment you ever make will have more than 2 of these 3 characteristics! So if safety and liquidity are your most desired characteristics for a particular sum of money, realize that you probably won't earn a high return on that money. At another time, if safety and a high return are your top concerns, then you'll probably have less liquidity, which means it may be difficult or impossible to get your money back before the investment matures. At still another point you may desire both a high return and liquidity, so it may be necessary to accept less safety, which means more risk. But if you diversify properly, you can acquire various holdings that provide you with your own optimum mix of these 3 characteristics in your investment portfolio.

So when someone says "more risk, more return," they're simply saying that most investments which have the potential to earn a high return are typically not investments that come with lots of guarantees. In Luke 14:28, Jesus encourages us to count the cost before we build. Like builders, investors should also count their costs and evaluate the risks before they commit to an investment.

Having the ability to earn consistently high returns is much like having professional athletic skills: if it were easy, everyone could do it! And just as there are baseball hitters who rarely hit home runs or strike out, but instead consistently hit singles and doubles, investors who take the same approach and save consistently while taking smaller, calculated risks, can often achieve remarkable results over time. But above all, as the Psalmist says, make sure that it's the Lord building your investment "house." Otherwise, your labor will be in vain (Psalm 127:1).

Next we'll discuss some ways that investors can each evaluate their own individual tolerance for risk.

"Paradigm Shifters—Action Points"

1) Consider many of the heroes in the Bible who took substantial risk: Noah, Abraham, David, Daniel, the disciples, the apostle Paul, and others. Since they heard God's instructions, were they really taking risks after all? I think I could make a case for both a "yes" and a "no." Also look at the risks Jonah encountered when he didn't follow God's instructions!

____

____

____

____

2) Not only do we have written accounts of how the Bible heroes dealt with risk, today we have virtually world-wide instantaneous communication capabilities. Technology allows us to have "counselors" and mentors around the world. These extra layers of communication offer us far more resources than were available thousands of years ago. But we must use these tools wisely: we must not rely on the tools more than we rely on time spent alone with God. And we must seek God first, above all others and before all others. I know I need to spend more time with God. I encourage you to build more of these appointments into your schedule also.

____

____

____

____

____

____

Day 10 Selah-Meditations

Proverbs 4:7

Wisdom is the principal thing; therefore get wisdom: and with all thy getting get understanding. (KJV)

The beginning of wisdom is: acquire wisdom; and with all your acquiring, get understanding. (NASB)

Above all and before all, do this: Get Wisdom! Write this at the top of your list: Get Understanding! (Message)

The beginning of Wisdom is: get Wisdom (skillful and godly Wisdom)! [For skillful and godly Wisdom is the principal thing.] And with all you have gotten, get understanding (discernment, comprehension, and interpretation). (Amplified)

Getting wisdom is the wisest thing you can do! And whatever else you do, develop good judgment. (NLT)

The first thing [is] wisdom -- get wisdom, And with all thy getting get understanding. (YLT)

Wisdom is supreme—so get wisdom. And whatever else you get, get understanding. (HCSB)

The beginning of wisdom [is], Get wisdom; and with all thy getting get intelligence. (Darby)

- Day 11 -

Today's WORD on Money™:
How to Decide if an Investment is Right for You

ask yourself which outcome would make you feel worse: would you have more regret about not buying an investment that earned a great return, or would you feel worse if you bought an investment that lost you a great amount of money?

Business people in the Bible did not all grow their wealth in the same way. So in the 21st century, how do you decide if an investment or an opportunity is right for you?

There are a number of ways to evaluate investment opportunities, but how do you determine your own tolerance for a particular investment? Proverbs 22:6 seems to indicate that we all have likes and dislikes, and God-given strengths that our parents and teachers can recognize and help us to grow. So <u>before anything else</u>, and before all of the steps that I'm showing you in this lesson, be sure you <u>ask God</u> to show you His purposes for you <u>and</u> for your investments.

We have several friends who specialize in helping people understand their gifts and God's plan for their lives, so please contact us if you would like to take some of the tests they offer. But until you take a personality test, let me share with you a couple of questions that I typically ask investors when I'm counseling them about various investments.

As we discussed yesterday, all investments have some combination of safety, liquidity, and rate of return. So when someone has moneys to invest, one of the questions I may ask them goes something like this: "With this money and at this point in your life, tell me which 2 of the 3 investment characteristics we discussed are most important to you right now? Once they tell me that it's liquidity and safety, safety and higher returns, or liquidity and higher returns, then I can begin to narrow down the types of investments that are better suited for their time frame, their temperament, and their tolerance for risk.

Here are some other great questions to ask yourself. If you're about to make a final decision, ask yourself which outcome would make you feel worse: would you have more regret about not buying an investment that earned a great return, or would you feel worse if you bought an investment that lost you a great amount of money? Many studies show that it feels <u>twice as bad</u> to <u>lose</u> a given amount of money as it <u>feels good</u> to <u>gain</u> that same amount of profit.

You can ask yourself a similar question when you have an investment that has performed well for you. Let's say you've made a 50% or 100% return so far, but you think that the investment still has the potential to continue growing in value. Which would make you feel worse: selling a profitable investment and then watching it gain much more in value, or holding the investment and watching your profit evaporate?

At this point, many people elect to take at least some of their profits off the table. That way, if the investment gains in value, they still make more money. But if the investment loses value, at least they locked in some of their profits before the downturn occurred. If you're <u>very</u> aggressive or <u>very</u> experienced, you can keep your winners and not sell anything until there is a fundamental change (e.g., a new CEO). We will discuss related strategies in a future segment, but the above two strategies have helped many people to invest more successfully.

"Paradigm Shifters—Action Points"

1) What has God taught you about making wise decisions? Find some way to spend time with people you admire, so that you can learn what God has taught them. You may have a Sunday School class or Life Group at your church that will help you learn more of God's ways. Or you may have a weekly breakfast or lunch meeting with one or more fellow-seekers. Be willing to be a little vulnerable. I guess I learned that lesson in sports. I couldn't improve unless I allowed myself to be coachable. Also, you need to be willing to "coach" others and pour into their lives. But use wisdom and speak in love. Make sure you point out more of what they're doing right, than of what they're doing wrong.

____

____

____

____

2) I heard Robert Lewis[1] make a distinction between mentoring and discipleship. Mentoring can be on any topic, but discipleship always has a spiritual purpose. But going back to our earlier lesson that pointed out the false distinction made between "sacred" and "secular," I believe that if you're looking to make better investment decisions, you can benefit from both mentoring and discipleship. Please share your comments with us about what you've learned on this topic.

____

____

____

____

[1] www.mensfraternity.com

Day 11 Selah-Meditations

(The enemy tries to make his trash look attractive to us, and in today's society, we're bombarded by it at almost every turn. These are good words to have memorized, so that we can "go on the offensive" against Satan's deceptions.)

Philippians 4:8-9
Finally, brethren, whatsoever things are true, whatsoever things are honest, whatsoever things are just, whatsoever things are pure, whatsoever things are lovely, whatsoever things are of good report; if there be any virtue, and if there be any praise, think on these things. Those things, which ye have both learned, and received, and heard, and seen in me, do: and the God of peace shall be with you. (KJV)

Finally, brethren, whatever is true, whatever is honorable, whatever is right, whatever is pure, whatever is lovely, whatever is of good repute, if there is any excellence and if anything worthy of praise, dwell on these things. The things you have learned and received and heard and seen in me, practice these things, and the God of peace will be with you. (NASB)

Summing it all up, friends, I'd say you'll do best by filling your minds and meditating on things true, noble, reputable, authentic, compelling, gracious—the best, not the worst; the beautiful, not the ugly; things to praise, not things to curse. Put into practice what you learned from me, what you heard and saw and realized. Do that, and God, who makes everything work together, will work you into his most excellent harmonies. (Message)

For the rest, brethren, whatever is true, whatever is worthy of reverence and is honorable and seemly, whatever is just, whatever is pure, whatever is lovely and lovable, whatever is kind and winsome and gracious, if there is any virtue and excellence, if there is anything worthy of praise, think on and weigh and take account of these things [fix your minds on them]. Practice what you have learned and received and heard and seen in me, and model your way of living on it, and the God of peace (of untroubled, undisturbed well-being) will be with you. (Amplified)

And now, dear brothers and sisters, one final thing. Fix your thoughts on what is true, and honorable, and right, and pure, and lovely, and admirable. Think about things that are excellent and worthy of praise. Keep putting into practice all you learned and received from me—everything you heard from me and saw me doing. Then the God of peace will be with you. (NLT)

As to the rest, brethren, as many things as are true, as many as [are] grave, as many as [are] righteous, as many as [are] pure, as many as [are] lovely, as many as [are] of good report, if any worthiness, and if any praise, these things think upon; the things that also ye did learn, and receive, and hear, and saw in me, those do, and the God of the peace shall be with you. (YLT)

Finally brothers, whatever is true, whatever is honorable, whatever is just, whatever is pure, whatever is lovely, whatever is commendable—if there is any moral excellence and if there is any praise—dwell on these things. Do what you have learned and received and heard and seen in me, and the God of peace will be with you. (HCSB)

For the rest, brethren, whatsoever things [are] true, whatsoever things [are] noble, whatsoever things [are] just, whatsoever things [are] pure, whatsoever things [are] amiable, whatsoever things [are] of good report; if [there be] any virtue and if any praise, think on these things. What ye have both learned, and received, and heard, and seen in me, these things do; and the God of peace shall be with you. (Darby)

From henceforth, brethren, whatever things be sooth, whatever things chaste, whatever things just, whatever things holy, whatever things able to be loved, whatever things of good fame, if any virtue, if any praising of discipline, think ye (on) these things, that also ye have learned, and taken, and heard, and seen in me. Do ye these things, and God of peace shall be with you. (Wycliffe NT)

- Day 12 -

Today's WORD on Money™: What is Good Stewardship?

. . . not only is giving a spiritual decision, so are earning, spending, saving and investing.

Since God expects us to make profitable financial investments, does that mean it's OK to invest in anything, as long as it's profitable? Let's look at what the Bible says.

First, let's define stewardship and profit. My friend and mentor Patrice Tsague defines Biblical Stewardship as "Exercising dominion over the natural resources of God to serve others while making a profit for the Kingdom of God." He defines Biblical Profit as "The spiritual and natural gain remaining after all costs are deducted from a business transaction, or from the total income of the business[1]."

So would it be acceptable if one of the stewards in the Parable of the Talents had doubled his money in a business that degraded women through pornography or prostitution? Would his Master have said "Well done", or would He have cast the steward into outer darkness along with the steward who was "wicked and lazy"?

More to the point, how should we as Christians respond when we learn that we own shares of companies that directly or indirectly condone pornography and other profitable but immoral activities? That's why my friend Frank Reynolds says that stewardship is not just about giving. It's about 100%, not just 10%, so not only is giving a spiritual decision, so are earning, spending, saving and investing.

I had a friend ask me if this book "teaches tithing". 10% is not what God is after. He wants our hearts, our undivided loyalty. Everything ultimately belongs to God, so we should be willing to do whatever He asks, whenever He asks us, in whatever amount He tells us. He promises that He will always meet our needs when we do this. (Philippians 4:19)

While I'm sure that some people have occasionally done some "good works" in an immoral business, I'm equally certain that the Bible teaches that God's greatest blessings will accrue to us when we do things God's way.

There are numerous examples of people who have ultimately triumphed or prospered by doing things God's way, even when they began in humble circumstances or positions. (cf., Joseph in Genesis 39 ff.; the widow and the oil in 1 Kings 17; Matthew 6:33 Amp., "But seek (aim at and strive after) first of all His kingdom and His righteousness (His way of doing and being right), and then all these things taken together will be given you besides.")

So then, we see that stewardship is not just about results, but is also about how we obtain them. (2 Tim. 2:1-3, 15; 2 Tim. 1:9; Col. 3; Philip. 4:8-9; Matt. 6:33) Stewardship involves not only financial considerations, but also spiritual considerations. If we are to let our light shine, as commanded in Matthew 5:16, then we must prayerfully consider how we treat those in authority over us, how we treat our co-workers, our employees, our customers, and our suppliers.

Jesus said in John 10:10 and in John 14:6 that He is life, so we must prayerfully study how to avoid promoting or condoning investments, products, actions, and conversations that do not minister life to those affected by what we do. Next we will share more of what God says about both morality and profit.

[1] For a more in-depth study on these principles, we recommend Nehemiah Project International Ministries' teaching, Biblical Entrepreneurship I, developed by our good friend and mentor, Patrice Tsague. (www.nehemiahproject.org)

"Paradigm Shifters—Action Points"

1) Take some time this week to reflect on how you earn, save, invest, spend, and give. If something is "holy," it is dedicated or set apart. How could you make each of these 5 activities holier in your life? Choose at least one of these areas to improve this week. I challenge all of us to work continually to improve in these 5 areas. I think that's one way we can go from "glory to glory."

____

____

____

____

2) Look at the other areas of your life: physical, mental, spiritual, social, and family. How could you be a better steward of what God has given you in each of these areas? But before all of my "action points" get to be too much of a "downer" for some of you, it's probably a good time for me to remind you of the difference between conviction and condemnation! <u>Conviction</u> leads to repentance, to positive change, and to life and life more abundant. <u>Condemnation</u> leads to death. At Jesus' trial before the crucifixion, Judas felt condemnation, so he hung himself. Peter felt conviction, so he changed and went on to win thousands to God's Kingdom. So don't beat yourself up when you identify something that you need to change. Thank God for the opportunity to grow and become all that He created you to be!

____

____

____

____

____

Day 12 Selah-Meditations

(This is a great passage to help us avoid living beneath our privileges, as children of the King!)

Ephesians 1:17 (read Ch. 1:16-23 for the context)

That the God of our Lord Jesus Christ, the Father of glory, may give unto you the spirit of wisdom and revelation in the knowledge of him: (KJV)

that the God of our Lord Jesus Christ, the Father of glory, may give to you a spirit of wisdom and of revelation in the knowledge of Him. (NASB)

But I do more than thank. I ask—ask the God of our Master, Jesus Christ, the God of glory—to make you intelligent and discerning in knowing him personally, (Message)

[For I always pray to] the God of our Lord Jesus Christ, the Father of glory, that He may grant you a spirit of wisdom and revelation [of insight into mysteries and secrets] in the [deep and intimate] knowledge of Him, (Amplified)

asking God, the glorious Father of our Lord Jesus Christ, to give you spiritual wisdom and insight so that you might grow in your knowledge of God. (NLT)

that the God of our Lord Jesus Christ, the Father of the glory, may give to you a spirit of wisdom and revelation in the recognition of him, (YLT)

[I pray] that the God of our Lord Jesus Christ, the glorious Father, would give you a spirit of wisdom and revelation in the knowledge of Him. (HCSB)

that the God of our Lord Jesus Christ, the Father of glory, would give you [the] spirit of wisdom and revelation in the full knowledge of him, (Darby)

that God of our Lord Jesus Christ, the Father of glory, give to you the spirit of wisdom and of revelation, into the knowing of him; (Wycliffe NT)

- Day 13 -

Today's WORD on Money™:
Should I Invest in a Company That Does This?

Since God wants to have a relationship with us, if we ask Him, He will show us both how to invest *and how to* serve *others, as part of His overall plan for us. (Jeremiah 29:11)*

What should we do if we're associated with a company whose activities are not in concert with our moral values? Do we "shake the dust off our feet" and walk away, or should we stay and try to persuade them to change their behavior? As with many issues, Christians don't all arrive at the same answers to these questions.

Obviously the undertaking we discussed yesterday is a serious task, and one that will involve regular review. Hebrews 4:12 teaches that God's Word is living and active, and 2 Corinthians 3:18 teaches that we go from glory to glory. Thus we will regularly need to examine our values as well as our portfolios. But are there times that we can admonish instead of condemning ourselves and others? (cf. Philemon v. 6 and 2 Timothy 2:2) I believe so. As we learn and grow, and as we walk in love, let us hope that others will see a difference in us and want what we have. Then the process can begin again, as God's love multiplies throughout the earth.

So how do we walk this out? Some companies offer "partner benefits," others sell tobacco, and others manufacture products that murder innocent lives. How do we as Christians minister life, and how do we demonstrate God's love to people without condoning their sins? What if a company is best known for making widgets, but it donates sizeable amounts of money to abortion clinics or to encourage lifestyles that lead to incurable diseases or premature deaths?

I have good friends who live out their commitment to Jesus by being adamant about not investing in any company that subsidizes any activity they believe is immoral. I have other good friends who look at Jesus' life and feel that since He "ate with sinners," they too have an obligation to own enough stock to attend annual shareholder meetings and speak out against corporate morality issues. I even have a few Christian friends who believe that <u>some</u> of these company policies are in line with the Beatitudes and therefore reflect mercy rather than approval of certain lifestyles!

I can't tell you what God's plan is for your life, but I do know one thing that all of my Christian friends have in common: they have prayed, they've studied God's Word, and they can articulate how they developed their own philosophies of stewardship and investment. So I admonish you to go and do likewise. Since God wants to have a relationship with us, if we ask Him, He will show us both how to <u>invest</u> and how to <u>serve</u> others, as part of His overall plan for us. (Jeremiah 29:11)

Farming illustrates this concept well: before planting, the farmer should ask the Lord what to plant, as well as when, where, and how to plant. In that process, the farmer clears the ground and prepares it to hold the seed. Then the farmer plants, waters (or prays for rain), and weeds, all in preparation for the harvest.

A farmer who plants lettuce uses different processes from a farmer who plants cotton, but both are farmers. Likewise, the decisions a business owner faces may differ from those an investor faces. But they can all be good stewards. And remember, God doesn't always do the same thing the same way. We are to depend on Him, and give Him the glory. Next we'll examine more investment characteristics.

"Paradigm Shifters—Action Points"

1) How many and what kind of seeds do you think God created you to sow? Where is the "good ground" that He wants you to tend? It could be your family, or it might be where you work, where you exercise, or where you fellowship. Ask God to reveal more to you, so that you can see more "100-fold" returns in every area of your life.

____

____

____

____

____

____

2) One of the workshops that we present to the donors of churches and ministries is called "Godly Investment Strategies." We go in-depth as to how Christians can determine when, where, and how they can invest in ways that will honor God. Here are a couple of links to help you learn more about this topic: http://www.stewardshippartners.com/stp2/index.asp?id=3-1 and http://kingdomadvisors.org/principles.html. I urge you to spend time evaluating how you can honor God by improving how and where you invest.

____

____

____

____

____

____

Day 13 Selah-Meditations

(I like to substitute my name and country in this verse. You may want to do the same.)

Ezra 7:10

For Ezra had prepared his heart to seek the law of the LORD, and to do it, and to teach in Israel statutes and judgments. (KJV)

For Ezra had set his heart to study the law of the LORD and to practice it, and to teach His statutes and ordinances in Israel. (NASB)

Ezra had committed himself to studying the Revelation of God, to living it, and to teaching Israel to live its truths and ways. (Message)

For Ezra had prepared and set his heart to seek the Law of the Lord [to inquire for it and of it, to require and yearn for it], and to do and teach in Israel its statutes and its ordinances. (Amplified)

This was because Ezra had determined to study and obey the Law of the Lord and to teach those decrees and regulations to the people of Israel. (NLT)

for Ezra hath prepared his heart to seek the law of Jehovah, and to do, and to teach in Israel statute and judgment. (YLT)

because Ezra had determined in his heart to study the law of the LORD, obey [it], and teach [its] statutes and ordinances in Israel. (HCSB)

For Ezra had directed his heart to seek the law of Jehovah and to do it, and to teach in Israel the statutes and the ordinances. (Darby)

Example:
This was because (<u>your name</u>) had determined to study and obey the Law of the Lord and to teach those decrees and regulations to the people of (<u>your country</u>).

So I would say it like this: "This was because Steve had determined to study and obey the Law of the Lord and to teach those decrees and regulations to the people of the United States." Depending on

God's purpose for your life, some of you may put "the world," or you may name several countries instead of naming only 1 country.

- Day 14 -

Today's WORD on Money™:
Can It be Attached?

. . . keep in mind that good stewardship entails diligence both in making a profit, and in protecting that profit from those to whom it does not belong.

We live in what many consider to be a litigious society. How can we protect what God has entrusted to our care? Let's look at a few ways.

This discussion is not meant to portray attorneys in a negative light. In fact, our firm works closely with several attorneys to make sure that our clients are protected from many types of litigation and risk. But the number of attorneys in the U.S. does increase the probability that you, your family, or your business could at some point be involved in some kind of legal action.

Many of the clients we advise are in professions that typically get sued more frequently than the general public. I am not an attorney, so I don't give legal advice. But we do often advise those who seek our advice to consult with an attorney about forming various trusts, entities, or partnerships in order to minimize the risk of losing assets because of litigation. Remember, stewardship is not just about money, it's about growing and protecting all that God entrusts to us in every area of our lives.

In addition to having good legal representation, there are other ways to protect assets. In many of the states in which we work, some types of insurance products cannot be attached in the event of litigation. So there have been times when we have recommended to clients that putting more money into a whole life insurance policy or into some kind of annuity would be much safer from a litigation standpoint than putting that same money into a mutual fund, or perhaps even into an insured CD or a guaranteed bond.

We believe that as a Christian, your ultimate source is God: not your money, not your job, not any of your other "stuff." But we as Christians <u>are</u> called to be good stewards. Stewardship requires that we be "***wise as serpents, and harmless as doves***" (Matthew 10:16). So it would not be wise to ignore the legal risks that can accompany success in business or in investing.

Likewise, if God gives you a witty invention, you would not be a good steward if you didn't file trademarks or patents to protect the ideas or products that God has entrusted to you. For example, until I had the copyright on this book, I even had my friends sign non-disclosure agreements before I let them read the manuscript.

So keep in mind that good stewardship entails diligence both in making a profit, and in protecting that profit from those to whom it does not belong.

“Paradigm Shifter—Action Points”

1) My former karate instructor, Danny Passmore, taught that martial artists aren't always “on the offensive.” In fact, that's why it's called “self-defense.” So protecting yourself may be as simple as backing up, walking away, or giving a “soft answer” that doesn't provoke or instigate a fight. This principle can also apply to your finances. Sometimes the best offense is a good defense. Don't be like Blondie, who tried to convince Dagwood that she saved $1000, when she actually spent $1500! Examine what you can do to manage your financial affairs with wisdom. One obvious defense that too many 21st century Americans need to implement is to have at least 3 months to 6 months of their living expenses saved up and available in some kind of liquid account. What can you do to improve your financial “self defense”?

____

____

____

____

2) What can you do “offensively” to protect the assets that God entrusts to you? One of the workshops we present is entitled “Provisional Risk Management.” Please spend some time with a competent advisor who can help you make provision against the risks that are specific to you in your personal, family, and work settings.

____

____

____

____

____

Day 14 Selah-Meditations

(I love the Message translation of this verse, so I listed it first. In fact, this verse has become our firm's second "theme verse," after 2 Timothy 2:2. I think it really describes how we should be "salt, light, and living water" wherever we are and whatever we do. Of course we can only do this with the help of the Holy Spirit.)

Matthew 13:52

(Jesus) said, "*Then you see how every student well-trained in God's kingdom is like the owner of a general store who can put his hands on anything you need, old or new, exactly when you need it.*" (Message)

Then said he unto them, Therefore every scribe which is instructed unto the kingdom of heaven is like unto a man that is an householder, which bringeth forth out of his treasure things new and old. (KJV)

And Jesus said to them, "Therefore every scribe who has become a disciple of the kingdom of heaven is like a head of a household, who brings out of his treasure things new and old." (NASB)

He said to them, Therefore every teacher and interpreter of the Sacred Writings who has been instructed about and trained for the kingdom of heaven and has become a disciple is like a householder who brings forth out of his storehouse treasure that is new and [treasure that is] old [the fresh as well as the familiar]. (Amplified)

Then he added, "Every teacher of religious law who becomes a disciple in the Kingdom of Heaven is like a homeowner who brings from his storeroom new gems of truth as well as old." (NLT)

And he said to them, `Because of this every scribe having been discipled in regard to the reign of the heavens, is like to a man, a householder, who doth bring forth out of his treasure things new and old.' (YLT)

"Therefore," He said to them, "every student of Scripture instructed in the kingdom of heaven is like a landowner who brings out of his storeroom what is new and what is old."
(HCSB)

And he said to them, For this reason every scribe discipled to the kingdom of the heavens is like a man [that is] a householder who brings out of his treasure things new and old. (Darby)

He saith to them, Therefore every wise man of [the] law in the kingdom of heavens [Therefore every writer taught in the kingdom of heavens], is like to an husbandman, that bringeth forth of his treasure new things and old. (Wycliffe NT)

- Day 15 -

Today's WORD on Money™: Should You Have a Mortgage?

. . . we sometimes tell clients this: "We think you should have your home paid off; we just don't think you should keep the money in your home."

Many clients tell us that they've always heard that they should pay off their mortgage. For some people, though, that may not be the safest thing to do.

But before I go any further, let me reassure you: if you can't sleep at night until your mortgage is fully paid, or if you interpret Romans 13:8 to mean that you should not have a mortgage, then by all means, I firmly believe you should pay off your mortgage!

Please understand--as a financial consultant, I believe that one of my duties is to help clients see the potential advantages and disadvantages of their financial decisions. So for those of you who want to make sure that what you believe to be true is in fact true, let's look at a couple of situations where it might be prudent for some people to keep a mortgage. First, you might not have enough money to make a lump-sum payment large enough to retire your mortgage. However, after you've heard today's information, if you would still like to pay off your mortgage as soon as possible, then be sure to study tomorrow's lesson.

Second, you might be close to retirement, out of work, or moving in the near future. I have met with people who had hundreds of thousands of dollars of equity in their home, but who had very little in liquid savings. These people were in a quandary. Some were faced with having to sell their home just so they could access their home equity and pay their bills. Some had been turned down for a home equity loan, because they were unemployed. In other words, what they thought was "their money" was inaccessible because their lender said "no." And even if the lender said "yes," what if home values were down and/or interest rates and payments were too high?

By the way, did you know that in many situations, if your lenders foreclose on your home, they are only obligated to sell your home for what you owe? In other words, if you have a $300,000 home, and you owe $100,000, then the bank only has to sell your home for $100,000, which could vaporize your $200,000 of "equity"! Few lenders might do this, but legally they could.

There are also people whose homes, though paid off, were destroyed by Hurricane Katrina in 2005. As of 2008, some had still not received a settlement for the value of their homes. That is one reason why we <u>sometimes</u> tell clients this: "We think you should have your home paid off; we just don't think you should keep the money <u>in</u> your home." So some clients may have a mortgage, but they have enough money in a tax-advantaged account to pay their home off at any time of <u>their</u> choosing.

Here's another example: let's say your home is worth $200,000. If I gave you a check today for $200,000, would you bury the check in your back yard? If you answered no, then you might not want to pay off your mortgage. Instead, you might want to put that money in a place where you could access it, should you need to pay off your mortgage. But if some unforeseen event occurs, you are not at the mercy of some lender who might not allow you to access "your" money.

Having said all that, though, for those who still think paying your home off early is the right choice <u>for you</u>, we'll share some strategies tomorrow that you probably haven't heard before.

"Paradigm Shifters—Action Points"

1) Do an internet search for the term "opportunity cost" or look it up on Wikipedia. Opportunity cost is something that your financial advisors should help you understand as it relates to the financial decisions you make. For example, we show clients that if they choose the wrong way to pay for their cars, it could make a $600,000+ difference in their net worth, over a 30 year to 40 year time frame. And you might be surprised by what is the best way to pay for vehicles! We'll share more on these strategies in our next book.

____

____

____

____

2) We recommend that you meet with financial advisors who can help you examine your lifestyle and your financial choices, so that you aren't being "penny wise and pound foolish." If you're like many people, you're not really comfortable sharing your personal information. But remember what Will Rogers said, "Everybody's ignorant . . . just about different things." So not sharing your information can be a bigger risk than sharing it with someone trained to advise you. Giving financial advice works much the same way as when doctors try to make sure they know your medical history and what other medications you take, before they recommend a new procedure or prescription.

____

____

____

____

____

3) In light of many events that have happened from 2007 to 2009, I believe it's important that we as Christians don't justify actions that have become acceptable by many in today's economic and legal climate. There are now legal ways for people or companies to rescind their commitments, whether it's getting out of a mortgage or the actions that a company takes after it files for bankruptcy. Back in Bible times, and even in the Old West, people gave their word, and a handshake was all that was needed. Today, some people look for ways to get out of agreements, pledges and promises they made <u>and</u> signed. As Christians, we should abide by Psalm 15:4 and "*swear to our own hurt*" rather than going back on our word.

Day 15 Selah-Meditations

(This is TRULY "as good as it gets," not some imitation or "TV Commercial" substitute.)

Psalm 16:11

Thou wilt shew me the path of life: in thy presence is fulness (sic) of joy; at thy right hand there are pleasures for evermore. (KJV)

You will make known to me the path of life; In Your presence is fullness of joy; In Your right hand there are pleasures forever. (NASB)

Now you've got my feet on the life path, all radiant from the shining of your face. Ever since you took my hand, I'm on the right way. (Message)

You will show me the path of life; in Your presence is fullness of joy, at Your right hand there are pleasures forevermore. (Amplified)

You will show me the way of life, granting me the joy of your presence and the pleasures of living with you forever. (NLT)

Thou causest me to know the path of life; Fulness of joys [is] with Thy presence, Pleasant things by Thy right hand for ever! (YLT)

You reveal the path of life to me; in Your presence is abundant joy; in Your right hand are eternal pleasures. (HCSB)

Thou wilt make known to me the path of life: thy countenance is fulness of joy; at thy right hand are pleasures for evermore. (Darby)

- Day 16 -

Today's WORD on Money™: What's the Most Efficient Way to Pay Off a Mortgage?

. . . a way that will allow you to pay off your home in 15 years or less, and with less money out-of-pocket *than the way most people do it.*

Yesterday we learned that some people sometimes might be better off to keep their home mortgage. If you don't believe that you're one of those people, but you presently lack the funds to pay cash for your home, what are some things you can do to pay it off soon as possible?

Some people think that in order to pay off their mortgage as soon as possible, they should make a big down payment, get the shortest term they can afford, then pay as much extra as they possibly can each month (or each year), along with their regular monthly payments. While this method has in fact worked for many people, it can have hidden costs. We believe that for the right person, there is another strategy that allows you to be "wise as a serpent, and harmless as a dove."

If you have enough discipline, this strategy allows you to pay off your mortgage AND to maximize the tax benefits of owning a home. First of all we need to remember how a mortgage works and how tax deductions are calculated. The first few years you have a mortgage, most of your monthly payment goes to pay interest, with very little going to reduce your principal. Near the end of your mortgage, most of your payment is going to pay principal, with little going to pay interest. So, for example, if you compare a 30-year mortgage with a 15-year mortgage, more of the 15-year payments go to pay off principal sooner. That's why the 15-year mortgage, which has higher monthly payments, pays the mortgage in 15 years, not 30 years.

The thing most people forget is that, unless you own a business, home mortgage interest is one of the few deductions left for the average taxpayer (unless you make a mid-six figure income or higher). What that means is that every time you pay more principal off, you reduce the amount of interest that accrues and that you can deduct. If you decrease your deductions, you increase your taxes. So many people pay off extra principal and think they're getting ahead. But then on April 15th, they have to reach back into their pocket and pay taxes with money they thought they had saved. Or they may actually have to borrow money to pay taxes, because their savings were used to decrease the principal on their mortgage! (Ever hear of 2 steps forward, 1 step back?)

We think there's a better way, a way that will allow you to pay off your home in 15 years or less, and <u>with less money out-of-pocket</u> than the way most people do it. For a disciplined person, we recommend that you get a 30-year mortgage, make a smaller down payment, and then create a tax-free "side fund" where you put the extra money that you would have paid, had you obtained a 15-year mortgage. Then when your side fund is large enough, write <u>one check</u> to pay off your mortgage in full. In other words, since you don't have to come up with more money to pay taxes, you can pay <u>off your home with less money</u> out of your pockets, typically as soon as or sooner than traditional strategies.

One translation of 2 Timothy 1:7 says that God has given us self discipline. The strategy we've just discussed certainly requires discipline, but if you are disciplined, this method helps to prevent those April 15th "surprises" which can occur when your deductions have disappeared. But don't use this method if you are not disciplined enough to build up a side fund that could ultimately be used to write that one check to pay off your mortgage. Tomorrow we'll discuss a strategy called "recasting," and a few possibilities for your "side fund."

"Paradigm Shifters—Action Points"

1) We should not ever make a financial or an investment decision based solely on the tax implications. But if you find that one of your previous strategies can be improved upon, then you may want to implement the "new and improved" strategy. For more information on how to avoid transferring wealth unknowingly and unnecessarily, please visit www.moneytrax.com.

____

____

____

____

____

____

2) Here's another question to ask yourself when considering whether or not to have a mortgage: if all mortgage terms contained the same amount of profit for the lender, how many different types of mortgages would be offered?!

____

____

____

____

____

____

Day 16 Selah-Meditations

(I especially like how the Amplified Version "amplifies" this verse.)

Matthew 6:33

But seek ye first the kingdom of God, and his righteousness; and all these things shall be added unto you. (KJV)

But seek first His kingdom and His righteousness, and all these things will be added to you. (NASB)

Steep your life in God-reality, God-initiative, God-provisions. Don't worry about missing out. You'll find all your everyday human concerns will be met. (Message)

But seek (aim at and strive after) first of all His kingdom and His righteousness (His way of doing and being right), and then all these things taken together will be given you besides. (Amplified)

Seek the Kingdom of God above all else, and live righteously, and he will give you everything you need. (NLT)

but seek ye first the reign of God and His righteousness, and all these shall be added to you. (YLT)

But seek first the kingdom of God and His righteousness, and all these things will be provided for you. (HCSB)

But seek ye first the kingdom of God and his righteousness, and all these things shall be added unto you. (Darby)

Therefore seek ye first the kingdom of God, and his rightwiseness, and all these things shall be cast to you. (Wycliffe NT)

- Day 17 -

Today's WORD on Money™: Where Can I Keep the Money?

. . . every investment has advantages and *disadvantages.*

In an effort to pay to Caesar only what belongs to him, what are some of the best tax-free places that you can use for a "side fund" to accumulate money for paying off your mortgage?

I often tell my clients that "every investment has advantages and disadvantages." Since we've previously discussed the disadvantages of having to pay too much in taxes, let's look at a few tax-advantaged ways to save money.

If you're about to get a home mortgage, you might ask the lenders if the mortgage will allow you to "recast." This strategy is a way for you to lower your mortgage payment each year, based upon the principal you've paid the previous year. If you then take the remainder amount that was being paid on your mortgage, and accumulate that amount into a tax-advantaged "side fund," you will eventually have a fund that is large enough to pay off your mortgage with one check. We previously discussed why it can be to your advantage to pay off your mortgage all at once, rather than with a series of smaller payments.

Whether or not you recast, there are several tax advantaged choices that you can make for a "side fund." We plan to write a book on investment choices soon, and our purpose for this book is not to recommend products, so for now we'll just mention 3 possibilities that some people have used in the past. You might use municipal bonds or a tax free money market fund. The individual bonds can be insured, and they have a definite rate of return, as well as a finite maturity date. This gives stability and predictability for the investor. One disadvantage of individual bonds, though, is that they generally only come in $5,000 increments. Also, you might not like your choice of maturity dates.

Tax free money market funds, on the other hand, are very liquid. They do not have a guaranteed rate of return or a finite maturity date. They can, however, be purchased or sold in almost any amount, any day the markets are open. Some funds can even be used much like a checking account.

Another side fund possibility for the right person is whole life insurance. If properly designed, insurance can help insulate assets from creditors and litigation[1], while also providing liquidity, use and control of the money you steward. The policy's death benefit could also be used to pay off a mortgage if the policy owner passes away.

[1] depending on your state of residence

"Paradigm Shifters—Action Points"

1) Tax evasion is illegal. Tax avoidance is legal, and it is even acceptable to the IRS. We have had clients try to save money by preparing their own tax returns. If you don't itemize, that may be adequate, but as you grow your wealth and employ a variety of strategies and investments, we believe that paying a CPA or an EA (Enrolled Agent) to do your taxes will be an investment that more than pays for itself. And just as there are attorneys who specialize in different areas of the law, CPA's and EA's may have special areas of expertise also. So, for example, if you are self-employed and your primary source for growing wealth is through real estate, you probably don't want to work with a tax preparer whose other clients all work for someone else and have no income from real estate investments.

____

____

2) If you have municipal bonds, be sure to do your homework on their safety. In the past few years, even some of the entities which insure bonds have experienced issues with their financial soundness.

3) To learn more about using insurance to fund purchases, see Nelson Nash's site, www.infinitebanking.org, where you can also order electronic and/or "hard copy" versions of his book, Becoming Your Own Banker.

Day 17 Selah-Meditations

(Some people don't even call out to God. To those of you who do call out, be sure to wait and listen for God's answer!)

Jeremiah 33:3

Call unto me, and I will answer thee, and show thee great and mighty things, which thou knowest not. (KJV)

'Call to Me and I will answer you, and I will tell you great and mighty things, which you do not know.' (NASB)

'Call to me and I will answer you. I'll tell you marvelous and wondrous things that you could never figure out on your own.' (Message)

Call to Me and I will answer you and show you great and mighty things, fenced in and hidden, which you do not know (do not distinguish and recognize, have knowledge of and understand). (Amplified)

Ask me and I will tell you remarkable secrets you do not know about things to come. (NLT)

Call unto Me, and I do answer thee, yea, I declare to thee great and fenced things -- thou hast not known them. (YLT)

Call to Me and I will answer you and tell you great and wondrous things you do not know. (HCSB)

Call unto me, and I will answer thee, and I will shew thee great and hidden things, which thou knowest not. (Darby)

- Day 18 -

Today's WORD on Money™:

"Garage Giveaways"

Thank God, our government still recognizes the value that faith-filled people and ministries bring to our society.

The Bible teaches how important it is for God's people to give. It's not only a privilege, it is a responsibility. But the benefits are far greater than most of us can imagine. If you are someone who thinks that our government is bloated and wasteful, you'll enjoy this lesson. Today we'll look at some ways that we can help the USA to become financially fit and trim!

My wife loves the Lord. God has given her many witty solutions to enhance our family's well-being and everyday routines. Back in the 1990's, she was cleaning out our closets, preparing to have a garage sale. My wife learned about garage sales from my mother, who was a garage sale expert! Mother knew how to buy, sell and dicker with the best! But on this particular day, as my wife was getting ready to put price tags on all of the garage sale items, she felt that the Lord wanted her not to put a price on anything. Instead, she felt that we were to give everything away for free!

We had so much fun with our first "garage giveaway," that we continue to have them. They have become a tradition with our family. At least once or twice a year, we put an ad in the paper. The ad says "garage sale", but when the doors go up, we make an announcement something like this: "How many of you have been here before? For those of you who are here for the first time, we do things a little differently from most garage sales. God has blessed us, so we want to be a blessing to you. You won't see price tags on anything, because everything is free! If you see something that you need, or if you know someone who needs it, you are welcome to take it."

We have had people actually break down and cry with joy at these events. When we started having them, we had only a few, well-used items, but God has increased our ability to give, and we now can often give away new things. We also give out Bibles, DVD's, and various tracts and booklets on spiritual topics. We can tell you from experience that it truly is more blessed to give than to receive.

Luke 6:38 tells us that when we give, it will be given back to us "*good measure, pressed down, shaken together, running over*." We don't give to get a blessing, but God has blessed our giving "exceedingly abundantly" beyond what we could ever have imagined (Ephesians 3:20). In fact, we enjoyed giving so much that we formed our own non-profit organization, 7 Cord Ministries.

Thank God, our government still recognizes the value that faith-filled people and ministries bring to our society. I encourage you to ask God for opportunities to give during your daily routines. You'll be glad you did. If just the Christians in America did this, can you imagine how many ineffective federal programs and inefficient taxes could be eliminated? Think about it! Our next few lessons will cover other topics related to gifting.

"Paradigm Shifters—Action Points"

1) What kind of "God idea" does the Lord want to give you? Listen, and let Him tell you! To get into the habit of listening, one of the first questions I have to ask myself is this, "Am I as eager to check my 'Inbox' with God as I am to check my 'Inbox' on Outlook, Facebook, Twitter, or Linked In?" How about you?

____

____

____

____

2) What need do you see that isn't being met? Almost all of us should become more "service-minded."

____

____

____

____

3) What gifts have you been given, which, if you use, will bless you and bless others?

____

____

____

____

Day 18 Selah-Meditations

(How would you like to have 40 more scriptures "hidden in your heart"? If so, pick your favorite translation below and memorize it. Watch how God's Word recharges you and how you grow in your walk with Jesus. Even if you don't memorize it, if you meditate on a verse throughout each day, over the next 40 days you will have cultivated a great habit!)

("A closed hand can't give, and it can't receive.")

Luke 6:38

Give, and it shall be given unto you; good measure, pressed down, and shaken together, and running over, shall men give into your bosom. For with the same measure that ye mete withal it shall be measured to you again. (KJV)

Give, and it will be given to you. They will pour into your lap a good measure--pressed down, shaken together, and running over. For by your standard of measure it will be measured to you in return. (NASB)

Give away your life; you'll find life given back, but not merely given back—given back with bonus and blessing. Giving, not getting, is the way. Generosity begets generosity. (Message)

Give, and [gifts] will be given to you; good measure, pressed down, shaken together, and running over, will they pour into [the pouch formed by] the bosom [of your robe and used as a bag]. For with the measure you deal out [with the measure you use when you confer benefits on others], it will be measured back to you. (Amplified)

Give, and you will receive. Your gift will return to you in full—pressed down, shaken together to make room for more, running over, and poured into your lap. The amount you give will determine the amount you get back. (NLT)

Give, and it shall be given to you; good measure, pressed, and shaken, and running over, they shall give into your bosom; for with that measure with which ye measure, it shall be measured to you again. (YLT)

Give, and it will be given to you; a good measure--pressed down, shaken together, and running over--will be poured into your lap. For with the measure you use, it will be measured back to you. (HCSB)

Give, and it shall be given to you; good measure, pressed down, and shaken together, and running over, shall be given into your bosom: for with the same measure with which ye mete it shall be measured to you again. (Darby)

Give ye, and it shall be given to you. They shall give into your bosom a good measure, and well-filled, and shaken together, and overflowing; for by the same measure, by which ye mete, it shall be meted again to you. (Wycliffe NT)

- Day 19 -

Today's WORD on Money™:
A Pile of Money on the Kitchen Table

. . . picture instead $3 million in cash sitting on a table in front of you.

What does the Bible teach about giving to our children or other descendants? Over the next few days, we'll review various ideas related to gifting.

Over the course of a lifetime, many people accumulate a wide variety of property and assets. Remember that in Week 2, we learned that God ultimately owns everything. With that in mind, here's a tip that Ray Lyne1 showed me. When deciding how to allocate assets to your heirs, first mentally convert everything to an amount. Let's say for example that if you added together all of your assets, you would come up with an amount of $3,000,000. So rather than picturing each individual asset, picture instead $3 million in cash sitting on a table in front of you. Then make a list of your heirs and of your favorite charities. Now decide how much you would like to give each name on your list. Furthermore, pretend that you have only 24 hours to give all of the money away. How much would you give to each name on the list?

After doing this exercise, many donors find that they are able to give more than they would have thought to ministries and charities, while still being generous to their descendants. Sometimes they also realize that some of their assets have appreciated to a value that is more than they want an individual heir to receive. So turning everything into a dollar amount helps them focus on what they really want to do. We tell our clients that what they bequeath is really the last investment and gifting decision that they get to make. As a result, many donors are able to make decisions more in line with what they believe God wants them to do.

Another concept that Ray Lyne shared with me is to help donors accomplish 4 goals with their estate design: 1) have adequate resources to last until God calls them home; 2) make sure that in Heaven, God tells them "Well done good and faithful steward" (Ray calls it "getting a hug from the Father"); 3) make sure that the heirs are still "hugging" each other 6 months after the donor goes to Heaven (It doesn't matter how much you save in taxes if your kids fight after you're gone!); 4) minimize all taxes, fees, and expenses.[1]

One other helpful bit of estate designing advice is to consider writing an ethical will. These date back to the Old Testament when the patriarchs spoke a blessing upon their descendants. Ethical wills are a way for you to pass along your values, not just your assets. Thus, even people who don't have a high net worth can bless their heirs by writing an ethical will. And if you prefer, you can read the ethical will to your heirs while you're still alive. Ethical wills can often help to heal old family wounds. For more information, visit www.ethicalwill.com. We'll continue our discussion on gifting strategies tomorrow.

[1] www.lifestylegiving.com As we say on our website, we have been richly blessed by studying under Ray Lyne. He knows more about Biblical stewardship than anyone else we have ever met. If we work on an estate design with you, the vast majority of the information we share with you will be what we have obtained from Ray, or from others whom Ray has mentored.

"Paradigm Shifters—Action Points"

1) What would you do differently with your children, if you had the chance to rear them again? Why not write it out and tell them in an ethical will? You can share with them the values and principles that you hold dear, and that you hope they will carry on. There are remarkable testimonies from both donors and heirs of how ethical wills have healed wounds in families who had given up even trying to speak to one another.

____

____

____

____

____

2) My family and I recently watched The Ultimate Gift again. If you are not familiar with this title, I encourage you to buy the book and the DVD immediately (if you don't have to finance it!). Senior adults will appreciate the values that are portrayed and taught, and youngsters may very well begin to adopt some of these values as their own. I highly recommend that you visit www.theultimategift.com and purchase at least 1 copy each of the book and the DVD. Or check with your local Christian book stores. You can also purchase these products online from major book retailers.

____

____

____

____

____

Day 19 Selah-Meditations

(See below. I believe this verse is so important for America today. I believe each of us should read this verse aloud, substituting our own name for "my people.")

2 Chronicles 7:14

If my people, which are called by my name, shall humble themselves, and pray, and seek my face, and turn from their wicked ways; then will I hear from heaven, and will forgive their sin, and will heal their land. (KJV)

and My people who are called by My name humble themselves and pray and seek My face and turn from their wicked ways, then I will hear from heaven, will forgive their sin and will heal their land. (NASB)

and my people, my God-defined people, respond by humbling themselves, praying, seeking my presence, and turning their backs on their wicked lives, I'll be there ready for you: I'll listen from heaven, forgive their sins, and restore their land to health. (Message)

If My people, who are called by My name, shall humble themselves, pray, seek, crave, and require of necessity My face and turn from their wicked ways, then will I hear from heaven, forgive their sin, and heal their land. (Amplified)

Then if my people who are called by my name will humble themselves and pray and seek my face and turn from their wicked ways, I will hear from heaven and will forgive their sins and restore their land. (NLT)

if my people who are called by my name humble themselves, and pray and seek my face and turn from their wicked ways, then I will hear from heaven and will forgive their sin and heal their land. (ESV)

and My people on whom My name is called be humbled, and pray, and seek My face, and turn back from their evil ways, then I -- I hear from the heavens, and forgive their sin, and heal their land. (YLT)

and My people who are called by My name humble themselves, pray and seek My face, and turn from their evil ways, then I will hear from heaven, forgive their sin, and heal their land. (HCSB)

and my people, who are called by my name, humble themselves, and pray, and seek my face, and turn from their wicked ways; then will I hear from the heavens, and forgive their sin, and heal their land. (Darby)

(Example: If I who am called by God's name will humble myself and pray and seek God's face, and turn from my wicked ways, then God will hear from heaven and forgive my sin and heal my land.)

- Day 20 -

Today's WORD on Money™:

The Greedy Farmer

. . . too many of the advisors in my profession tell their clients to do what the fool did in Luke chapter 12: tear down their barns and build bigger barns.

For years, Americans have repeatedly had to watch the destructive impact of sin and greed on the economy, on businesses, and on our financial markets. When I was growing up on the farm, my father said it this way: "Steve, most farmers aren't greedy. They just want the land next to theirs." Today we'll examine how the Bible answers the question "How much is enough?"

I grew up in Oklahoma. My father grew up during the Great Depression in the 1930's, when Oklahoma was in the midst of the "Dust Bowl." While his heart was tender toward the things of God, he sometimes had a gruff exterior. But he shared much wisdom with me as I grew up, and as I was privileged to work with him during my 20's and 30's. One day when we were working on the farm, I recounted some "great idea" I'd read about in one of my financial newsletters. As I finished, I said, "You should do this; you can write it off." In his own inimitable way my dad replied, "Son, you gotta have somethin' to write it off from first."

And he was right. Too often, modern day Americans get ahead of themselves, many times for the sake of pride or appearance. They either bite off more than they can chew financially, or they devise elaborate strategies that are only appropriate for someone with much greater wealth than they have. And if and when some of these strategies <u>do</u> become appropriate, too many of the advisors in my profession tell their clients to do what the fool did in Luke chapter 12: tear down their barns and build bigger barns.

I believe that it's time for us to become "rich toward God." Ultimately, He owns everything, including our very lives. So Biblical financial advisors should help clients to determine what a full barn looks like in each client's circumstances. Once someone's barn is full, then if God gives them more than that, instead of tearing their barns down, they should ask God what He wants them to do with that extra wealth. Now that's laying up treasure in heaven—treasures that will last forever!

Notice I didn't say that it's evil to have a full barn. In fact, as we've already discussed, we should take our stewardship responsibilities seriously. But when we truly seek God's wisdom, He will let us know how big our respective barns should be. And stewardship includes not only earning, saving, and investing, but also praying about when, where, and how much we should be giving.

There are an infinite number of ways to acquire wealth, and to distribute it. Just make sure that your advisor will truly help you to do what you believe God wants you to do with the wealth God has entrusted to you.

Too often for selfish reasons, advisors have either intentionally or unintentionally tricked their clients into building a bigger barn, sticking a cross on the side of the barn, and then keeping the contents inside the barn, rather than distributing the wealth in the way God intended.

Next, we'll continue to learn what the Bible says about giving.

"Paradigm Shifters—Action Points"

1) What does a "full barn" look like for you? If you don't know, take the time to seek what God wants to reveal to you in this matter. People who don't do this often wonder why "another dollar" is never enough, and why "more stuff" brings only temporary peace and satisfaction.

____

____

____

____

____

2) Pick one thing in your life that you've allowed to get too complicated. Here's one thing I've noticed in my life, and in the lives of many others: so-called time-saving devices don't really allow us to relax more or have more "free time." All most of us do is try to multi-task and pack more into every new little crevice of time that becomes available. Then people wonder why they feel stressed. . . . Just as we need to decide what a "full barn" looks like, we also need to determine what a "full schedule" looks like. I know that too often I have let work take too big a percentage of my time. Pray about how you're stewarding all that God gave you in every area of your life.

____

____

____

____

____

3) What is something you could do to be "rich toward God"? I've had Luke 6:38 memorized for over 20 years now, and I highly encourage you to internalize it as well. "Give, and it will be given to you. A good measure, pressed down, shaken together and running over, will be poured into your lap."

____

____

____

____

____

Day 20 Selah-Meditations

Philippians 2:5 (For additional insight, also read verses 6-8)

Let this mind be in you, which was also in Christ Jesus: (Who, being in the form of God, thought it not robbery to be equal with God: But made himself of no reputation, and took upon him the form of a servant, and was made in the likeness of men: And being found in fashion as a man, he humbled himself, and became obedient unto death, even the death of the cross.) (KJV)

Have this attitude in yourselves which was also in Christ Jesus, (NASB)

Think of yourselves the way Christ Jesus thought of himself. (Message)

Let this same attitude and purpose and [humble] mind be in you which was in Christ Jesus: [Let Him be your example in humility:] (Amplified)

You must have the same attitude that Christ Jesus had. (NLT)

For, let this mind be in you that [is] also in Christ Jesus, (YLT)

Make your own attitude that of Christ Jesus, (HCSB)

For let this mind be in you which [was] also in Christ Jesus; (Darby)

And feel ye this thing in you, which *was* also in Christ Jesus; (Wycliffe NT)

- Day 21 -

Today's WORD on Money™:

Harvest Time!

Rather than returning to God the wealth that He has entrusted to us while we're alive, we pay attorneys huge sums of money so that when we die, our children can get God's money*!*

There's nothing like harvest time on a farm. If you've never farmed, it's hard for me to describe to you the feelings of satisfaction and gratitude as you realize how God has blessed the work of your hands. But as a parent, I have at least some of those same feelings as I watch my children growing up. So for the next 2 lessons, we're going to discuss inheritances.

When it's harvest time, you do whatever it takes to get your crop to market or stored up in the barn. But at the same time, you try to avoid being wasteful. Christian farmers know that they ultimately have to answer to God for how they were stewards of the land and the crops that God entrusted to them.

But stewardship isn't limited only to farmers. All of us will eventually stand before God to answer how we cared for and distributed everything that He entrusted to our care. Clients often hear me talk about minimizing taxes, fees, and expenses. So let me share a story with you that I've often shared with clients.

Suppose that after a career of over 30 years in the marketplace, you have redirected your efforts, and you now spend most of your time volunteering, so you entrust the management of your savings to me. Each month I send you and your spouse a check which covers your living expenses. I manage your accounts so that they continue to grow. Over the years, as your cost of living increases, I am able to increase the size of your monthly income.

After living a long, full life, you go Home to be with the Lord in Heaven. The month following your death, your wife calls me to ask where her monthly check is. I tell her that I am no longer able to provide her a monthly income from your savings, because I gave your money to MY children! How would you feel if I did that to your family?

Friends, here's my point—don't we do the same thing with God's money? Rather than returning to God the wealth that He has entrusted to us while we're alive, we pay attorneys huge sums of money so that when we die, <u>our children can get God's money</u>!

Now don't get me wrong: I'm not saying that we shouldn't leave any wealth to our children. Proverbs 13:22 is one of many verses that counsels otherwise. But I <u>am</u> saying that too many of us at best "tip" God when we die, just as we "tip" him when the offering plate goes by. (And some of us don't even "tip" God, we "stiff" Him!!) If we truly believe that God owns everything, then we need to take what has become commonplace in terms of estate design and turn it upside down.

For more information on Godly estate designs, visit <u>www.lifestylegiving.com</u> or contact our firm. Tomorrow we'll continue our discussions of how to receive, care for, and give back the things that God entrusts to us.

"Paradigm Shifters—Action Points"

1) The Amplified version of the Bible translates the word "Selah" as "pause, and calmly think of that!" Why not pause and calmly think about the difference between stewardship and ownership. How could your life be better if you became more of a steward and less of an owner?

____

____

____

____

____

____

2) Have you invested any time asking God to show you how He wants you to bequeath the assets that you now steward for Him? (Of course, this assumes that He hasn't asked you to give something away already.)

____

____

____

____

____

____

Day 21 Selah-Meditations

Mark 12:17 (Matthew 22:21, Luke 20:25)

And Jesus answering said unto them, Render to Caesar the things that are Caesar's, and to God the things that are God's. And they marvelled at him. (KJV)

And Jesus said to them, "Render to Caesar the things that are Caesar's, and to God the things that are God's." And they were amazed at Him. (NASB)

Jesus said, "Give Caesar what is his, and give God what is his." Their mouths hung open, speechless. (Message)

Jesus said to them, Pay to Caesar the things that are Caesar's and to God the things that are God's. And they stood marveling and greatly amazed at Him. (Amplified)

"Well, then," Jesus said, "give to Caesar what belongs to Caesar, and give to God what belongs to God." His reply completely amazed them. (NLT)

Jesus said to them, "Render to Caesar the things that are Caesar's, and to God the things that are God's." And they marveled at him. (ESV)

and Jesus answering said to them, 'Give back the things of Caesar to Caesar, and the things of God to God'; and they did wonder at him. (YLT)

Then Jesus told them, "Give back to Caesar the things that are Caesar's, and to God the things that are God's." And they were amazed at Him. (HCSB)

And Jesus answering said to them, Pay what is Caesar's to Caesar, and what is God's to God. And they wondered at him. (Darby)

And Jesus answered and said to them, Then yield ye to the emperor those things that be the emperor's; and to God those things that be of God. And they wondered of him. (Wycliffe NT)

- Day 22 -

Today's WORD on Money™:

Eat the Grapes, But Don't Kill the Vines. . . .

. . . there are 3 things that people can do with God's "grape vines": be good stewards of them, try to give them away to someone who is not the rightful owner, or chop them down and use them for firewood.

America has been blessed with many freedoms. We are free to take an idea and turn it into a business that creates both jobs and wealth. But how do you prevent taxes from instantly vaporizing wealth that took decades to build?

One of my mentors is Ray Lyne of www.lifestylegiving.com. Ray knows more about Biblical stewardship and estate design than anyone else I've met. He tells a 7 minute "parable" about an apple orchard. With Ray's permission, my friend Frank Reynolds re-tells the story by describing a vineyard. With Frank's permission, I will briefly summarize the vineyard story.

In the beginning, God created the grape vine. He told people to care for it, and to return 10% of the grapes to God, so that the people would always remember that God owns the vineyard. As the number of people and vineyards multiplied, conflicts began to arise. So God placed government over the vineyards. But it was expensive to protect the people and to settle their disputes. So the government began to require people to give up some of each grape harvest in order to pay these government "expenses." We'll call these expenses an "income tax."

Eventually a government came along that did not know God. We'll call this government "Caesar." Caesar did not recognize God as the owner of the vineyards, and he kept demanding more and more of the grapes. So some people decided to sell their vineyards and buy grape packing houses instead. But when the people sold the vineyards, Caesar declared a "capital gains" tax and cut down ¼ of the vines.

Later, when some of the people who tended the vineyards died, Caesar cut down ½ of their vines, calling it an "estate tax." So the people found a solution. They began to allow charities to pick the grapes for a time. Sometimes they even donated an entire vineyard to charity. Caesar even encouraged these donations because he realized that charities often did a better job at helping the poor and needy than did many of Caesar's own agents. And the people realized that getting a tax deduction was much better than allowing Caesar to destroy the vines, since God sometimes wanted the people's children to continue tending the vineyard.

What's more, Caesar even gave the people a tax deduction to build fences that would keep Caesar from destroying the vines. These deductions provided the people with extra income which was used to grow assets that they could donate to charity or pass along to their heirs. When the right fences were built, Caesar could not invade the vineyards even after the people's children, grandchildren, and great grandchildren went to Heaven. The people also realized that their fences protected God's vineyards from the effects of divorce and litigation.

The point of our "vineyard story" is this: there are 3 things that people can do with God's "grape vines": be good stewards of them, try to give them away to someone who is not the rightful owner, or chop them down and use them for firewood. We encourage you to work with advisors who will strive to help you be a good steward.

"Paradigm Shifts—Action Points"

1) Isn't it interesting that some people, who would never dream of not paying their taxes, say that they can't afford to tithe or to give? So let me get this straight—they fear the IRS more than they fear the King of the Universe? I'm <u>not</u> saying that you should not pay

your taxes. But I am saying that until you acknowledge that it is God who "*gives you power to get wealth*" (Deuteronomy 8:18), you will never experience God's best in all areas of your life (which includes having enough money to pay your bills).

____

____

____

____

____

2) In situations where both governmental and charitable agencies are present, why do you think that churches and ministries so often do a more effective job than government? I remember a Paul Meyer speech that I heard years ago. He said that using taxes to run government agencies was like giving yourself a blood transfusion from your right arm to your left arm, and spilling ½ of the blood on the way from one arm to the other!

____

____

____

____

____

Day 22 Selah-Meditations

Matthew 7:11

If ye then, being evil, know how to give good gifts unto your children, how much more shall your Father which is in heaven give good things to them that ask him? (KJV)

"If you then, being evil, know how to give good gifts to your children, how much more will your Father who is in heaven give what is good to those who ask Him!" (NASB)

As bad as you are, you wouldn't think of such a thing. You're at least decent to your own children. So don't you think the God who conceived you in love will be even better? (Message)

If you then, evil as you are, know how to give good and advantageous gifts to your children, how much more will your Father Who is in heaven [perfect as He is] give good and advantageous things to those who keep on asking Him! (Amplified)

So if you sinful people know how to give good gifts to your children, how much more will your heavenly Father give good gifts to those who ask Him. (NLT)

If you then, who are evil, know how to give good gifts to your children, how much more will your Father who is in heaven give good things to those who ask him! (ESV)

if, therefore, ye being evil, have known good gifts to give to your children, how much more shall your Father who [is] in the heavens give good things to those asking him? (YLT)

If you then, who are evil, know how to give good gifts to your children, how much more will your Father in heaven give good things to those who ask Him! (HCSB)

If therefore *ye*, being wicked, know [how] to give good gifts to your children, how much rather shall your Father who is in the heavens give good things to them that ask of him? (Darby)

Therefore if ye, when ye be evil men, know how to give good gifts to your sons, how much more your Father that is in heavens shall give good things to men that ask him? (Wycliffe NT)

- Day 23 -

Today's WORD on Money™:
529 Plans--Estate Planning or College Funding?

please remember that the best inheritances include wisdom and instruction, not just knowledge and money.

Over the last decade or so, 529 plans have become a popular way to help pay for children's and grandchildren's education expenses. I think 529 plans can be an excellent estate planning tool, but they are not always the best way to pay for college.

First, there are spiritual issues that I believe Christians should consider when funding their children's education. In college, I was exposed to alternative lifestyles and ideologies that crippled my spiritual growth for over a decade. But thank God for redeeming that time, and for allowing me to use those experiences to prevent others from being deceived as I was. Because of my experiences, I believe that Christians should first and foremost seriously consider who will be teaching their children, and the doctrines espoused in the classrooms. Do you think the Hebrews would have allowed Canaanites to teach their children? Wisdom is not acquired only in schools.

Next, you should consider if it is in your children's best interest to have their education given at no financial cost to them. Some children will waste this gift, while others will appreciate it, so use discernment. Even for wealthy parents, it may be better for some children to have a part-time job while they attend college, in order to prove that they are serious about getting their degree.

In contrast, I know of some parents who calculate what they would have spent on college, and then invest that sum within an entity that the child cannot touch before, say, age 60. Assuming a fair rate of return, that lump sum should grow to an amount at least equal to what the child would otherwise have saved by age 60. So if the student has a skill or interest that won't be significantly enhanced by attending college, some parents may want to consider this alternative strategy.

Here's another issue: the money in 529 accounts cannot be used for all college expenses. If used for non-stipulated expenses, proceeds can be taxed. Also, if the child gets a scholarship, and the parents have no one else who needs the 529 funds, then there are penalties for withdrawing the money if it is not used for designated education expenses. However, wealthier clients do like the fact that when they place money into a 529 account, the money is now <u>not</u> considered part of their estate. This has a double benefit: potential estate taxes are reduced, while the client maintains some control over how and when the money is spent on the student's college expenses.

So if the people we advise decide against establishing 529 accounts, we explore other options. We will discuss those options in our next book. In the meantime, as you ponder Proverbs 13:22 and how to leave an inheritance for your children's children, please remember that the best inheritances include wisdom and instruction, not just knowledge and money.

"Paradigm Shifters—Action Points"

1) If you were a (grand) parent with a student entering college this year, which <u>2002 college funding strategy</u> do you think you would feel better about now:

a) Putting $55,000 into stocks, mutual funds, or a 529 plan;
b) Putting $55,000 into a whole life insurance policy;
c) Putting $55,000 into CD's or government bonds;
d) Putting $55,000 into various types of real estate investments;
e) Putting $55,000 into tax free bonds;
f) Putting $55,000 into a variable annuity;
g) Putting $55,000 into precious metals or other "alternative investments";
h) Putting $55,000 into a tin can in your backyard?

Why?

____

____

____

What if, for example, you had put $55,000 into choice "b", and then loaned yourself $25,000 from the policy, to purchase smaller amounts of any or all of the remaining choices? Would "paying yourself back" be preferable to borrowing from a third party? Are there strategies that allow you to have assets, cash, <u>and</u> a death benefit? Which would you prefer for the same amount of money: one asset or multiple assets? For those of you with younger (grand) children, does this question help you re-think your choices?

In other words, are there ways to "recycle" assets, so that you can diversify and multiply the wealth that you steward . . . ?

Ecclesiastes 11:6 (NLT) says this:

> *"Plant your seed in the morning and keep busy all afternoon, for you don't know if profit will come from one activity or another—or maybe both."*

2) What can you do as a parent to help your children become good stewards?

____

____

____

____

____

Day 23 Selah-Meditations

(If people have a mental image of a stern God waiting to punish us the moment we make a mistake, then they haven't read this verse.)

Jeremiah 29:11

For I know the thoughts that I think toward you, saith the LORD, thoughts of peace, and not of evil, to give you an expected end. (KJV)

'For I know the plans that I have for you,' declares the LORD, 'plans for welfare and not for calamity to give you a future and a hope.' (NASB)

I have it all planned out—plans to take care of you, not abandon you, plans to give you the future you hope for. (Message)

For I know the thoughts and plans that I have for you, says the Lord, thoughts and plans for welfare and peace and not for evil, to give you hope in your final outcome. (Amplified)

For I know the plans I have for you," says the Lord. "They are plans for good and not for disaster, to give you a future and a hope. (NLT)

For I know the plans I have for you, declares the LORD, plans for welfare and not for evil, to give you a future and a hope. (ESV)

For I have known the thoughts that I am thinking towards you -- an affirmation of Jehovah; thoughts of peace, and not of evil, to give to you posterity and hope. (YLT)

For I know the plans I have for you"—[this is] the LORD's declaration—"plans for [your] welfare, not for disaster, to give you a future and a hope. (HCSB)

For I know the thoughts that I think toward you, saith Jehovah, thoughts of peace, and not of evil, to give you in your latter end a hope. (Darby)

- Day 24 -

Today's WORD on Money™: Educational Inheritance Planning

. . . there are ways to leave a financial inheritance for both the Kingdom and *for your descendants!*

Until shortly before World War II in America, the main inheritance that many children received was in the form of farm land. But since the war, more children work in careers that are related to their personal preferences, instead of working where they were born, or doing the same type of work their parents did. Today we will study how these changes affect inheritance decisions.

When America was still an agrarian economy, the best tangible inheritance that a child could receive was farm land. Land grew crops and helped meet the lifelong needs of a farmer and his family. But America is no longer an agrarian economy, even though our farmers' productivity is among the highest in the world. So now if a child inherits land, it will rarely be his or her primary source of livelihood.

Instead, education has become the predominant way for parents to help their children "get ahead." Over a 40 year period of time, it is estimated that many college graduates will earn at least one million dollars more than high school graduates will earn during that same time frame. This statistic has implications both for today's parents and for today's children.

For the children, if they will have the discipline to save a large portion of this extra income instead of consuming it, then when they are ready to "retire" or to redirect, they should have a substantial amount of assets accumulated—enough for all but their most extravagant needs throughout the remainder of their lives.

For the parents, they may realize that helping their children to attend college has at least as much value in today's economy as a gift of land had in the agrarian economy[1]. At that point, the parents can have more freedom to follow what God directs them to do with the remaining assets that they steward for God, who is ultimately the true Owner.

For example, the parents may believe that they should leave most of their remaining assets to be used for Kingdom and charitable work. If so, then they can make the appropriate bequests without feeling that they have shortchanged their children. And if the children have had this perspective explained to them, they can be thankful that they received their inheritance at any early age—an educational inheritance that should benefit them for the rest of their lives. But as we'll soon learn, there are ways to leave a financial inheritance both for the Kingdom and for your descendants!

Remember, though, the key to all of this is to follow God's directions. He may tell some of you that you are to withhold funds for education altogether. He may tell others that you should give your heirs a large portion of what God has entrusted to you. The important thing is truly to seek God's direction, so that when you stand before the Lord, you can hear Him say, "Well done, good and faithful steward." You don't want Him to ask, "Why did you give My money to your children?"

[1] Please refer to our previous lesson on whether or not children should attend college.

"Paradigm Shifters—Action Plans"

1) Are you more interested in sending your children to college because of how it will appear to others if they don't go, or because you and your children have heard from God how, when, where and why they should attend? I don't know about you, but when I was 18, I had very little ability to heed God's wisdom or follow His directions. If your (grand) children are still young, teach them how to communicate with God. It's worth more than <u>any</u> diploma from <u>any</u> school. And when your children know why they're going to college, they're much less likely to "squeeze" a 4 year program into 7 years!

I'm not saying that we shouldn't ever change courses or careers. In fact, we've already discussed "retirement" versus "redirection." But when I finally discovered in my 40's that one of my key callings is in the financial arena, it was as a result of asking God last, in desperation, instead of first, in dedication. God has graciously allowed me to minister to others because of the painful experiences I put myself through. But there were 15+ years when I thought I ran the show, so there were many people that I could have served and didn't, or that I could have served more effectively. But thank God for His mercy! Much like the Apostle Paul said, I believe that I'm putting those childish things behind me, and that I'm focusing on God's purposes for me in the time that remains.

____

____

____

2) What can you do to <u>internalize</u> and habitually act on the fact that everything good that you have came from God, and that you are to manage it wisely?

____

____

____

Day 24 Selah-Meditations

(Don't try to do it all yourself! It's not about us anyway—it's about God.)

Proverbs 11:14

Where no counsel is, the people fall: but in the multitude of counsellors there is safety. (KJV)

Where there is no guidance the people fall, but in abundance of counselors there is victory. (NASB)

Without good direction, people lose their way; the more wise counsel you follow, the better your chances. (Message)

Where no wise guidance is, the people fall, but in the multitude of counselors there is safety. (Amplified)

Without wise leadership, a nation falls; there is safety in having many advisers. (NLT)

Where there is no guidance, a people falls, but in an abundance of counselors there is safety. (ESV)

Without counsels do a people fall, And deliverance [is] in a multitude of counsellors. (YLT)

Without guidance, people fall, but with many counselors there is deliverance. (HCSB)

Where no advice is, the people fall; but in the multitude of counsellors there is safety. (Darby)

- Day 25 -

Today's WORD on Money™:
How Many Legs Does Your Chair Have?

For those donors who are Kingdom-minded, there are some great alternatives to selling. In fact, ministries are the last, best hope for these donors.

As we continue our studies on giving, we want to review some of the many forms that gifts can take. And we want to remember that God loves cheerful givers[1]. Let's look at how to become cheerful, systematic, proactive givers.

A number of people are concerned that the Social Security system is in trouble. What many church and ministry leaders don't yet realize is that if Social Security is in trouble, many ministries are in trouble. Why? Most ministries receive almost all of their revenue from their donors' disposable income. That's like trying to sit in a chair that only has 1 leg—very uncomfortable and likely to fall!

Let me share with you the other 3 legs that we believe all ministries should have. In addition to gifts of income, there are gifts of assets. The good news for donors is that there are a number of ways to give to your favorite ministries while at the same time increasing your income. For example, many donors have highly appreciated assets like land, property, art or investments that pay little or no income. Selling these assets might result in huge tax bills for the donors. For those donors who are Kingdom-minded, there are some great alternatives to selling. In fact, ministries are the last, best hope for these donors. Asset gifts can often provide donors with both tax deductions and increased income. And donors have the satisfaction of seeing their gifts go to work while they're still alive.

The next type of giving is planned giving. These gifts can also help to fund Kingdom-related projects. Donors can choose whether they would like to receive income now or later, and they can also choose when they would like their favorite ministries to receive proceeds from the gifts. Planned gifts can dramatically accelerate ministries' ability to fully fund their visions.

Last, there are estate gifts. These are gifts that are usually made upon the death of the donor(s). Christian estate gifts are typically the result of a Godly estate design. They often involve gifts from wills, trusts, or insurance policies. And while these gifts may be made with the "stroke of a pen," they can often exceed what the donors have previously given during their entire lifetime.

Not only the very wealthy, but also people who may consider themselves middle class can often make these kinds of gifts. I've seen the satisfaction on their faces when they realize they are able to give back to God far more than they had ever imagined. For more information on Godly estate designs, or to explore how and why you or your favorite ministry should fulfill all that God has envisioned for you, visit www.kingdomadvisors.org/roadblocks_min.html. You can be a cheerful giver, and you can help your favorite ministry to sit on a "chair" with 4 legs instead of 1!

[1] "Let each one [give] as he has made up his own mind and purposed in his heart, not reluctantly or sorrowfully or under compulsion, for God loves (He takes pleasure in, prizes above other things, and is unwilling to abandon or to do without) a cheerful (joyous, 'prompt to do it') giver [whose heart is in his giving]." (2 Corinthians 9:7, Amplified)

"Paradigm Shifters—Action Points"

1) What can you do to become a more cheerful, proactive, systematic giver?

____

____

____

____

2) Can you imagine how different the U.S. could be if all of the Christians in America stewarded God's assets (e.g., physical, spiritual, mental, and financial) so well that they didn't need to apply for Social Security?! Do you think that non-Christians might be interested in how that came about?!

____

____

____

____

3) Think about this statement: "Giving is an antidote to greed."

____

____

____

____

____

Day 25 Selah-Meditations

Matthew 28:19-20 (The "Great Commission")

Go ye therefore, and teach all nations, baptizing them in the name of the Father, and of the Son, and of the Holy Ghost: Teaching them to observe all things whatsoever I have commanded you: and, lo, I am with you always, even unto the end of the world. Amen. (KJV)

"Go therefore and make disciples of all the nations, baptizing them in the name of the Father and the Son and the Holy Spirit, teaching them to observe all that I commanded you; and lo, I am with you always, even to the end of the age." (NASB)

"Go out and train everyone you meet, far and near, in this way of life, marking them by baptism in the threefold name: Father, Son, and Holy Spirit. Then instruct them in the practice of all I have commanded you. I'll be with you as you do this, day after day after day, right up to the end of the age." (Message)

"Go then and make disciples of all the nations, baptizing them into the name of the Father and of the Son and of the Holy Spirit, teaching them to observe everything that I have commanded you, and behold, I am with you all the days (perpetually, uniformly, and on every occasion), to the [very] close and consummation of the age. Amen (so let it be). (Amplified)

Therefore, go and make disciples of all the nations, baptizing them in the name of the Father and the Son and the Holy Spirit. Teach these new disciples to obey all the commands I have given you. And be sure of this: I am with you always, even to the end of the age." (NLT)

"Go therefore and make disciples of all nations, baptizing them in the name of the Father and of the Son and of the Holy Spirit, teaching them to observe all that I have commanded you. And behold, I am with you always, to the end of the age." (ESV)

'having gone, then, disciple all the nations, (baptizing them -- to the name of the Father, and of the Son, and of the Holy Spirit, teaching them to observe all, whatever I did command you,) and lo, I am with you all the days -- till the full end of the age.' (YLT)

"Go, therefore, and make disciples of all nations, baptizing them in the name of the Father and of the Son and of the Holy Spirit, teaching them to observe everything I have commanded you. And remember, I am with you always, to the end of the age." (HCSB)

Go [therefore] and make disciples of all the nations, baptising them to the name of the Father, and of the Son, and of the Holy Spirit; teaching them to observe all things whatsoever I have enjoined you. And behold, *I* am with you all the days, until the completion of the age. (Darby)

Therefore go ye, and teach all folks, baptizing them in the name of the Father, and of the Son, and of the Holy Ghost; teaching them to keep all things, whatever things I have commanded to you; and lo! I am with you in all days, into the end of the world. (Wycliffe NT)

- Day 26 -

Today's WORD on Money™: Ministering to the Wealthy?

I know it's hard for us to understand that someone Who even knows the names of all the stars is really concerned about the minute details of our lives, but it's true.

Some people think that ministry only occurs when you help someone who's "down and out." Helping those in obvious trouble is certainly one way to minister, but there are many other ways Christians can be involved in "ministry." As we learned early in our series, even business should be treated as a form of ministry. So today, let's examine what ministry really is.

Alan Ross, a mentor of mine who lives in Atlanta, says that the 3 things God values are salvation, discipleship, and service. Ephesians 4:11 mentions 5 offices that God ordained to edify and minister to the body of Christ: apostles, prophets, evangelists, pastors and teachers.

My friend Frank Reynolds defines ministry this way: **"Christian ministry is helping people move from where they are to where they need to be, which ultimately is closer to God."** This definition frees us up to work wherever we're called. There are certainly many hurting people who have no money, but a quick review of recent headlines reveals that rich and famous people are also hurting. I don't want to sound pious, so please hear my heart on this: I believe that one of the calls that God has placed on my life is to minister to people who are wealthy.

Let me share with you just a few of the concerns that wealthy people have:

1) Uncertainty about how long they will live;
2) Lack of wisdom as to how they should provide for their spouse and other heirs;
3) Uncertainty as to how much wealth they should or should not leave to their heirs;
4) The complexity of our tax and legal systems;
5) What is the best way to pass along a business to future generations?

Our firm helps people to find solutions for these and many other concerns. But there are other Biblical financial advisors besides those in our firm. In fact, one of our future lessons will provide some guidelines on how to find a Biblical advisor.

But do not solely depend on the advice of any one human being. Proverbs tells us that it is wise to have multiple counselors, and there is no substitute for time spent with God in praise, worship, prayer, and Bible study. In my own quiet times, some of my best insights from God have come from cross-referencing verses electronically, which for me is easier to do than turning actual pages in a book. But guess what? God will even show you what method of Bible study works best for you. There's just one catch: you have to ask Him!

The Bible says that God cares for us. I know it's hard for us to understand that someone Who even knows the <u>names</u> of <u>all</u> the stars is really concerned about the minute details of our lives, but it's true.

<u>I challenge you</u> to ask God for the answer to some problem you haven't been able to solve, and that you've neglected to bring to God. Then <u>truly, patiently listen</u>. His reply may surprise you, but He <u>will</u> answer.

"Paradigm Shifters—Action Points"

1) Jesus didn't look up to the rich, and He didn't look down on the poor. He wasn't intimidated to eat in Zaccheus' lavish home, and he didn't hesitate to lay hands on a leper. I don't know that I'm there yet. Are you? I'm praying for those who read or hear this book. Will you pray for me?

____

____

____

____

2) Let us hear from you with ways that God has shown you how to walk closer to Him, whether it's a method of Bible study, a specific routine, or how you pray, praise and worship God.

____

____

____

____

3) What are some ways that you have ministered? What successes or victories have you had? What could you do to minister more effectively and more often?

____

____

____

____

Day 26 Selah-Meditations

(How would you like to have 40 more scriptures "hidden in your heart"? If so, pick your favorite translation below and memorize it. Watch how God's Word recharges you and how you grow in your walk with Jesus. Even if you don't memorize it, if you meditate on a verse throughout each day, over the next 40 days you will have cultivated a great habit!)

Luke 12:6-7

Are not five sparrows sold for two farthings, and not one of them is forgotten before God? But even the very hairs of your head are all numbered. Fear not therefore: ye are of more value than many sparrows. (KJV)

"Are not five sparrows sold for two cents? Yet not one of them is forgotten before God. Indeed, the very hairs of your head are all numbered. Do not fear; you are more valuable than many sparrows." (NASB)

"What's the price of two or three pet canaries? Some loose change, right? But God never overlooks a single one. And he pays even greater attention to you, down to the last detail—even numbering the hairs on your head! So don't be intimidated by all this bully talk. You're worth more than a million canaries." (Message)

Are not five sparrows sold for two pennies? And [yet] not one of them is forgotten or uncared for in the presence of God. But [even] the very hairs of your head are all numbered. Do not be struck with fear or seized with alarm; you are of greater worth than many [flocks] of sparrows. (Amplified)

"What is the price of five sparrows—two copper coins? Yet God does not forget a single one of them. And the very hairs on your head are all numbered. So don't be afraid; you are more valuable to God than a whole flock of sparrows." (NLT)

Are not five sparrows sold for two pennies? And not one of them is forgotten before God. Why, even the hairs of your head are all numbered. Fear not; you are of more value than many sparrows. (ESV)

Are not five sparrows sold for two assars? And one of them is not forgotten before God, but even the hairs of your head have been all numbered; therefore fear ye not, than many sparrows ye are of more value. (YLT)

Aren't five sparrows sold for two pennies? Yet not one of them is forgotten in God's sight. Indeed, the hairs of your head are all counted. Don't be afraid; you are worth more than many sparrows! (HCSB)

Are not five sparrows sold for two assaria? And one of them is not forgotten before God. But even the hairs of your head are all numbered. Fear not therefore, ye are better than many sparrows. (Darby)

Whether five sparrows be not sold for two halfpence [for two farthings]; and one of them is not in forgetting before God? But also all the hairs of your head be numbered. Therefore do not ye dread; ye be of more price than many sparrows. (Wycliffe NT)

- Day 27 -

Today's WORD on Money™:
Is Stewardship the Same Thing as Giving?

If we are to accomplish God's good plans for us (Jer. 29:11), we need to realize that stewardship deals with all of every aspect of our lives, not just 10% of our finances.

Many people think that stewardship and giving mean the same thing. But not every giver is a steward, although every steward is a giver. What does God's Word teach us about stewardship?

Let's say that one Sunday you've tried to summarize for people in your congregation some of what you've learned in our Today's WORD on Money™ series. You end your presentation by saying this, "Be sure not to miss next week's service. It's going to be "Stewardship Sunday." Do you think you'll have more people attend your church next week, or less? If you answered "more," you are part of a rare congregation! Most people believe that stewardship is a code word for "giving." But the truth is, God doesn't just care about 10% of our money. He cares about 100% of everything. If we are to accomplish God's good plans for us (Jer. 29:11), we need to realize that stewardship deals with all of every aspect of our lives, not just 10% of our finances.

Misunderstanding our stewardship responsibilities leads to all kinds of problems. We'll highlight just two in today's study. As our first example, think about this: poor physical stewardship leads to pre-mature deaths, and to many diseases that were rare or non-existent 100 years ago. Some Christians live healthier lifestyles than non-Christians, but even many Christians don't pray about what or how much they put into their bodies.

I believe that the whole issue of health care coverage in America should begin with the proposition that each American must take some responsibility for the stewardship of his or her own health. No wonder health care costs have skyrocketed! Should those who take responsibility for their health be expected to pay for the problems which result from the physical, dietary[1], alcohol- and drug-related, or sex-related excesses of others?

God says this in Deuteronomy 30:19, "*I have set before you life and death, blessing and cursing. Therefore choose life. . . .*" Just as God has given me freedom, I believe my fellow Americans should have the freedom to choose any lifestyle they want. But I expect them to accept responsibility for the consequences of their choices. And while Christians should be merciful, should they be financially or politically obligated to pay for others' poor choices? No more so than those who make poor choices should be forced to choose healthy lifestyles. If someone else wants freedom to choose, then I should have the corresponding freedom to refuse to pay for their poor choices. Neither of us should have it both ways! We don't force smokers to quit smoking, but they have to live with ostracisms, mostly because of the health problems that smoking can cause. Shouldn't we treat other indulgences, behaviors and addictions in similar ways?

Here's another stewardship issue. If Christians fully utilized our spiritual, human and financial endowments, we wouldn't have to use "gimmicks" or "beg for bucks" to fund our ministries' visions. Activities could be held for fellowship instead of as bait to raise money. Christians shouldn't need an excuse to give. Others might see we're different and seek advice on how to be fully funded without golf tournaments, car washes, and bake sales! Some of the best insights I've seen on how and why ministries should minister to their donors can be found at http://www.kingdomadvisors.org/roadblocks_min.html.

Lastly, here are two final examples that I encourage you to study on your own: 1) my friend Frank Reynolds says that the Parable of the Talents should instead be called, "Serving the Intentions of the Master." What do you think? 2) What do you conclude about your own stewardship when you study Luke 6:38? I hope these brief discussions stimulate all of you to invest some quality time this week in developing your own personal stewardship theology.

[1] For help with weight loss, see Homer Owen's site: www.homerowen.com

"Paradigm Shifters—Action Points"

1) Are you a giver, a steward, or neither? Why?

____

____

____

____

____

2) Do you agree with the "tough love" stance of not subsidizing unhealthy lifestyles? If so, contact your local, state and national elected officials. What do you think about former Governor Mike Huckabee's statement that America doesn't have a health <u>care</u> problem, we have a <u>health</u> problem? What will <u>you</u> do, <u>starting today</u>, to become healthier?

____

____

____

____

____

3) How could your favorite ministries make better use of their donors' spiritual, human and financial endowments? How do you think doing so would impact these ministries? Do you think that if a ministry has a huge endowment, it means that their staff and supporters need less faith to do what God is calling them to do? Can you only live by faith if you limit your financial resources??

____

____

____

____

____

4) What if a donor wanted to bequeath $1,000,000 to a ministry—would a ministry that "walks by faith" refuse the gift? If not, why would they not proactively minister to their donors, instead of "voluntarily" sitting on a "one-legged chair"? And could this ministry be preventing donors from fulfilling God's call on the donors' lives as well? For some possible answers to these and other questions, visit http://www.kingdomadvisors.org/roadblocks_min.html. Here are a couple of the issues this link addresses: a) ***If ministry leaders really have faith, is fund-raising necessary?*** b) ***Is "discipling givers" merely interesting, or is it my Biblical responsibility?***

____

____

____

____

____

Day 27 Selah-Meditations

Matthew 25:21

His lord said unto him, Well done, thou good and faithful servant: thou hast been faithful over a few things, I will make thee ruler over many things: enter thou into the joy of thy lord. (KJV)

"His master said to him, 'Well done, good and faithful slave. You were faithful with a few things, I will put you in charge of many things; enter into the joy of your master.' " (NASB)

"His master commended him: 'Good work! You did your job well. From now on be my partner.' " (Message)

His master said to him, Well done, you upright (honorable, admirable) and faithful servant! You have been faithful and trustworthy over a little; I will put you in charge of much. Enter into and share the joy (the delight, the blessedness) which your master enjoys. (Amplified)

"The master was full of praise. 'Well done, my good and faithful servant. You have been faithful in handling this small amount, so now I will give you many more responsibilities. Let's celebrate together!" (NLT)

His master said to him, 'Well done, good and faithful servant. You have been faithful over a little; I will set you over much. Enter into the joy of your master.' (ESV)

And his lord said to him, Well done, servant, good and faithful, over a few things thou wast faithful, over many things I will set thee; enter into the joy of thy lord. (YLT)

"His master said to him, 'Well done, good and faithful slave! You were faithful over a few things; I will put you in charge of many things. Share your master's joy!' " (HCSB)

His lord said to him, Well, good and faithful bondman, thou wast faithful over a few things, I will set thee over many things: enter into the joy of thy lord. (Darby)

His lord said to him, Well be thou, good servant and faithful; for on few things thou hast been true, I shall ordain thee on many things; enter thou into the joy of thy lord. (Wycliffe NT)

- Day 28 -

Today's WORD on Money™:

3 World Views

Making either the "left" or the "right" one's primary worldview causes distortions that will ultimately result in unfairness, failed human endeavors and failed systems of government.

Is anyone besides me ready for the political bickering in America to tone down? I understand that disagreements won't end, since we have Freedom of Speech, but now most "civil discussions" have been replaced by shouting matches, with all participants rudely interrupting each other. That is not how our parents and grandparents taught us to behave! Please allow me to share some insights into how we can complete instead of compete.

I wish I could share this word picture with every U.S. citizen who is now or is soon to be of voting age. Picture an equilateral triangle with 2 corners at the bottom and 1 at the top, like a pyramid.[1] Let's label the top corner "Transcendent." Call the bottom left corner "Left," and the bottom right corner "Right." Now let's explore 3 major worldviews.

The "Transcendent" worldview originated in the Judaic culture and now resides mainly in the Judeo-Christian religious sector. Proponents of this worldview hold that God or some creative force is the ultimate authority or owner. "Transcendent" proponents believe that funding should come from donations.

The "Left" worldview originated with the Greeks and now resides in the public sector. Proponents of this worldview hold that government should be the ultimate authority or owner. "Left" worldview proponents believe that funding should come from taxes.

The "Right" worldview originated with the Romans and now resides in the private sector. Proponents of this worldview hold that acquisitors or entrepreneurs should be the ultimate authorities or owners. "Right" worldview proponents believe that funding should come from investments and/or profits.

So the "right" proponents say something like, "If it's to be, it's up to ME," while the "left" says, "If it's to be, it's up to WE," and the "transcendent" says, "If it's to be, it's up to HE (God)." But further study of God's Word reveals that all 3 views contain truth. In fact, <u>if and only if</u> the "transcendent" view is your "Big Picture," then the 3 views can, and in fact, <u>must</u> work together. Making either the "left" or the "right" one's primary worldview causes distortions that will ultimately result in unfairness, failed human endeavors and failed systems of government.

However, if (and only if) we acknowledge that God is the ultimate authority, then the 2 other perspectives are necessary components: 1) from the "right," we realize that each of us needs to do our part in God's Kingdom; 2) from the "left," we realize that we all need to work together as the Body of Christ to bring about God's purposes for this planet, and for each person on earth. But when any political party tries to take God out of the equation, that party is ultimately doomed to fail. If God is omitted and the "left" prevails, socialism or communism eventually result and ultimately fail when they provide no individual incentives. Likewise if God is omitted and the "right" prevails, then as unbridled capitalism results, kindness and mercy are lacking, and pure greed eventually brings the country to ruin.

I don't know about you, but in recent years I have sadly watched many "solutions" from both the "left" and the "right" continue to fester, because God was not included in the solution. These observations were an additional incentive for me to write this book.

Next, we'll discuss how crucial it is for legislators to understand the difference between <u>fairness</u> and <u>justice</u>.

[1] This worldview illustration comes from the book Faith and Finances by Gary Moore.

"Paradigm Shifters—Action Points"

1) If you are tired of political arguments that occur when you're at the "water cooler" at work, or sipping coffee at your favorite hangout, memorize the "3 Worldviews" triangle story above. Let us know how it works for you. Then teach this strategy to others. If each of you would teach 2 other people this year, and then they each taught 2 more, and so on, can you imagine how different (and better!) the whole political/campaign process would be?

____

____

____

____

____

2) Meditate on ways that you can use the "3 Worldviews" story not only to help people re-think their political viewpoints, but also their spiritual perspectives. The "Transcendent" viewpoint is not limited to the Judeo-Christian perspective. For example, it might also be applied by someone with an "intelligent design" point of view.

____

____

____

____

____

Day 28 Selah-Meditations

(How would you like to have 40 more scriptures "hidden in your heart"? If so, pick your favorite translation below and memorize it. Watch how God's Word recharges you and how you grow in your walk with Jesus. Even if you don't memorize it, if you meditate on a verse throughout each day, over the next 40 days you will have cultivated a great habit!)

(Too often we condemn ourselves instead of accepting God's forgiveness. Oddly enough, this can actually result from our pride, trying to DO something to earn what only Jesus could pay for.)

2 Corinthians 5:21

For he hath made him to be sin for us, who knew no sin; that we might be made the righteousness of God in him. (KJV)

He made Him who knew no sin to be sin on our behalf, so that we might become the righteousness of God in Him. (NASB)

How? you ask. In Christ. God put the wrong on him who never did anything wrong, so we could be put right with God. (Message)

For our sake He made Christ [virtually] to be sin Who knew no sin, so that in and through Him we might become [endued with, viewed as being in, and examples of] the righteousness of God [what we ought to be, approved and acceptable and in right relationship with Him, by His goodness]. (Amplified)

For our sake he made him to be sin who knew no sin, so that in him we might become the righteousness of God. (ESV)

for him who did not know sin, in our behalf He did make sin, that we may become the righteousness of God in him. (YLT)

He made the One who did not know sin to be sin for us, so that we might become the righteousness of God in Him. (HCSB)

Him who knew not sin he has made sin for us, that *we* might become God's righteousness in him. (Darby)

God the Father made him sin for us, which knew not sin, that we should be made [the] rightwiseness of God in him. (Wycliffe NT)

- Day 29 -

Today's WORD on Money™: The Difference between Fairness and Justice

. . . here's the truly critical question: was it fair *or* just *that Jesus died on the cross for you and me?*

Have you noticed how often the word "fair" is mentioned by politicians? Actually, fairness should not be our litmus test when deciding on a course of action or for whom we should vote.

As you study the Bible, you'll begin to learn that God is a God of justice, not necessarily fairness. If you're like I was when I first realized this, you might be surprised, even upset or disappointed. How many times have we all said something like, "that's not fair," or how often have we taken up some "righteous cause" for someone who was being treated unfairly? What we too often fail to realize is that in this fallen, imperfect world, there is no way for *everyone* to be treated fairly. As soon as we make a concession to one group, someone else will perceive that concession as unfair, or they'll want a better concession for themselves. This "one-upmanship" has become rampant in politics—every legislator tries to obtain some kind of favor for his or her constituency.

Let's look at the Parable of the Talents, beginning in Matthew 25, verse 14. As we see how each of the three servants handles the wealth entrusted to them by their master, we begin to see justice, not fairness. The most obvious illustration of this is when the master gave the lazy servant's talent to the servant who already had 10 talents. If politicians who were ignorant of Biblical wisdom were in charge of the talents, not only might they have given the lazy servant's talent to the servant with 4 talents, they might also have made the servant with 10 talents give ½ of his talents to the lazy servant, so that each servant would then have 5 talents. But we would never ask the 4.0 students to give 1.0 to the 2.0 students, so that everyone could have a 3.0 Grade Point Average. So why should we do that with money? I'm not saying that poor people are lazy; I'm saying that no social program can do all that God can do. In fact I've seen Godly clients live prosperous lives, even though their incomes were very small. Likewise I've seen people wither without God, in spite of large incomes. But aside from these points, here's the truly critical question: was it <u>fair</u> or <u>just</u> that Jesus died on the cross for you and me?

These examples are not intended to say that we as Christians should not be merciful. Indeed, the parable of the unjust steward teaches us that since we've been forgiven such a great debt, we live out our gratitude to God by forgiving others. The Lord's Prayer says, "Forgive us our debts as we forgive our debtors." But many Christians confuse mercy and forgiveness with fairness. What did Jesus say when the woman caught in adultery was brought to Him? First He made sure that the men knew that they were unqualified to judge her, since they also were imperfect sinners. But then, as He forgave the woman, He didn't tell her to continue living in the same manner as she had before she met Him. No, he said "Go and sin no more."

Most government and non-faith based programs of which I'm aware essentially say, "Now that's OK sweetie, we know you didn't mean it. So we'll just give you another chance." Another chance may actually be what is needed, but most of these programs don't equip their clients with the proper tools *or* motives to effect any meaningful, long-term change in their lives.

My friend Patrice Tsague used to run a "secular" non-profit organization. After he allowed Jesus to become the Lord of his life, Patrice realized that what he had been teaching wasn't truly changing the lives of his drug-dealing clients. Instead, his information was only helping them to sell more drugs! That's why you often see higher success rates in many faith based programs than in the programs of their secular counterparts. Chuck Colson, Mac Gober, Mike Barber and many other Christian organizations help their clients to change from the inside out, not from the outside in.

"Paradigm Shifters—Action Points"

1) Think back on times when you were treated "unfairly." Can you forgive? If you can't, then don't expect to be forgiven of the times when you treated someone else unfairly.

____

____

____

____

____

____

2) Plan now what you can say and do in your daily routines that will exemplify justice and mercy, realizing that you can't always be "fair." Remember though, sometimes "letting someone off the hook" may not help them in the long run. As a case in point, do an internet search of the name "Mercury Morris," and read what he says about how his athletic abilities caused people to be too lenient with him, which eventually led to his spending 3 years in prison. Or look at all the problems O.J. Simpson has had over the last 10+ years.

____

____

____

____

____

____

Day 29 Selah-Meditations

1 Thessalonians 4:11

And that ye study to be quiet, and to do your own business, and to work with your own hands, as we commanded you; (KJV)

and to make it your ambition to lead a quiet life and attend to your own business and work with your hands, just as we commanded you, (NASB)

Stay calm; mind your own business; do your own job. You've heard all this from us before, but a reminder never hurts. (Message)

To make it your ambition and definitely endeavor to live quietly and peacefully, to mind your own affairs, and to work with your hands, as we charged you, (Amplified)

Make it your goal to live a quiet life, minding your own business and working with your hands, just as we instructed you before. (NLT)

and to aspire to live quietly, and to mind your own affairs, and to work with your hands, as we instructed you, (ESV)

and to study to be quiet, and to do your own business, and to work with your own hands, as we did command you, (YLT)

to seek to lead a quiet life, to mind your own business, and to work with your own hands, as we commanded you, (HCSB)

and to seek earnestly to be quiet and mind your own affairs, and work with your [own] hands, even as we charged you, (Darby)

and to aspire to live quietly, and to mind your own affairs, and to work with your hands, as we instructed you, (Wycliffe NT)

- Day 30 -

Today's WORD on Money™: When Did Commerce Begin?

As we see how God gives unique gifts to each of us, we also begin to see His plan for redemption and then restoration.

The word "money" is in the title of our book. One of the reasons for money is to pay for the exchange of goods and services. The buying and selling of goods is known as commerce. Have you ever thought about when commerce began?

In Genesis 2 we read that after God created man, He put man in the garden. There man could eat from all of the good food available. We also read about gold and other minerals in the land to which the Pishon River flowed. Then beginning in verse 15 we read that God assigned work to Adam: he was to care for the garden, and he named all of the animals that God created. So Adam worked before he sinned. But although he worked, he had no need for money. He had everything he needed without having to pay someone else.

But in Genesis 3 we see a dramatic turn of events. The serpent lies and Eve and Adam buy into the lie. This changes their relationship with God and with their environment. Now they will have to sweat and struggle. Their work will be hard because the ground is cursed, and childbirth will be painful. Chapter 3 is also when the first animal was killed to provide clothing for humans.

So while work began in Genesis chapter 2, commerce did not begin until chapter 3. As work became harder and less productive, people did not have time to produce all of their own needs. In chapter 4 we see specializations begin to develop. Verse 2 tells us that Abel was a shepherd, while Cain was a farmer. By the end of the chapter, several other professions are named: there are ranchers, various types of musicians, iron workers and artisans.

Over time there were prophets, poets, fishermen, warriors, kings and priests. So ponder with me for a moment just a couple of the many levels of meaning in the Bible, which has far more levels than any other literary work. As we see how God gives unique gifts to each of us, we also begin to see His plan for redemption and then restoration. As we accept what Jesus did and surrender our abilities back to God's purposes, we bless and we are blessed, interconnecting our uniqueness with that of billions of others, allowing God to weave this earthly-yet-eternal, human-yet-spiritual tapestry. Just as our bodies don't function right without all the parts, so the church can't fully function unless each of us does what we were created to do. But as each of us in our own unique way "lifts Him up", using our God-given abilities to honor Him, still others are drawn to His Kingdom, and the entire process begins again.

Ephesians 4:16 (Amplified) says it this way: *"For because of Him the whole body (the church, in all its various parts), closely joined and firmly knit together by the joints and ligaments with which it is supplied, when each part [with power adapted to its need] is working properly [in all its functions], grows to full maturity, building itself up in love."*

The New Living Translation says this: *"He makes the whole body fit together perfectly. As each part does its own special work, it helps the other parts grow, so that the whole body is healthy and growing and full of love."*

I hope it doesn't take persecution to bring about cooperation, but when the various parts of the church organism (not the organization) truly and fully begin to work together, then more people will want what we have. Our way of life will lift Jesus up, and people will be drawn to Him. An interesting paradox is that many who talk more about the Kingdom than about salvation actually see more salvations than do those who limit their efforts to "beating people over the head" with the salvation message!

"Paradigm Shifters—Action Points"

1) Examine your work habits and your relationships with friends, family and co-workers. What are some ways that you can rely on God more, instead of trying to "do it all by yourself"? How will this improve your results and your health, for example?

____

____

____

____

____

____

2) When you look at the past, if you've truly repented for things you regret, now you can be thankful for God's forgiveness, which can release you to help others avoid making the same mistakes you made. Based on your past, what are some ways that you can minister to others? In my case, one way I am able to minister is that I can speak from experience about the inability of "wine, women and song" and "get rich quick" schemes to bring the true lasting joy that only God can bring.

____

____

____

____

____

____

Day 30 Selah-Meditations

(This is one of those "one finger pointing at you, 3 fingers pointing back at me" verses.)

1 John 4:18

There is no fear in love; but perfect love casteth out fear: because fear hath torment. He that feareth is not made perfect in love. (KJV)

There is no fear in love; but perfect love casts out fear, because fear involves punishment, and the one who fears is not perfected in love. (NASB)

There is no room in love for fear. Well-formed love banishes fear. Since fear is crippling, a fearful life—fear of death, fear of judgment—is one not yet fully formed in love. (Message)

There is no fear in love [dread does not exist], but full-grown (complete, perfect) love turns fear out of doors and expels every trace of terror! For fear brings with it the thought of punishment, and [so] he who is afraid has not reached the full maturity of love [is not yet grown into love's complete perfection]. (Amplified)

Such love has no fear, because perfect love expels all fear. If we are afraid, it is for fear of punishment, and this shows that we have not fully experienced his perfect love. (NLT)

There is no fear in love, but perfect love casts out fear. For fear has to do with punishment, and whoever fears has not been perfected in love. (ESV)

fear is not in the love, but the perfect love doth cast out the fear, because the fear hath punishment, and he who is fearing hath not been made perfect in the love; (YLT)

There is no fear in love; instead, perfect love drives out fear, because fear involves punishment. So the one who fears has not reached perfection in love. (HCSB)

There is no fear in love, but perfect love casts out fear; for fear has torment, and he that fears has not been made perfect in love. (Darby)

Dread is not in charity, but perfect charity putteth out dread [but perfect charity sendeth out dread]; for dread hath pain. But he that dreadeth, is not perfect in charity. (Wycliffe NT)

- Day 31 -

Today's WORD on Money™:

What Happens to Good Intentions?

. . . if you want to be a better steward in every aspect of life, don't give fear any place in your life.

I've heard it said that we judge others by their actions, but we judge ourselves by our good intentions! Have you ever wondered why our stewardship isn't as good as our intentions? I have.

2 Timothy 1:7 says that God has not given us a spirit of fear, but of power, of love, and of a sound mind, or of self discipline. So if God didn't give us fear, where did it come from? Obviously, from the enemy, who loves it when we're afraid. One way fear comes is by doubting that the things of God are truly more powerful than the lies and tricks of the enemy.

But Philippians 2:8-11 says this: *(Jesus) humbled Himself by becoming obedient to the point of death—even to death on a cross. For this reason God also highly exalted Him and gave Him the name that is above every name, so that at the name of Jesus every knee should bow—of those who are in heaven and on earth and under the earth — and every tongue should confess that Jesus Christ is Lord, to the glory of God the Father.* (HCSB)

I heard one preacher say it like this: "Fear has a name. Depression has a name. Overweight has a name. Diabetes has a name. But God's Word says that Jesus' name is above every name. We just need to start acting on the power of that name." When we are afraid, it can usually be traced back to the ultimate fear, which is the fear of death. I've found that speaking God's Word out loud helps me, whenever I'm confronted by something that would try to make me afraid, whether it's a TV ad, a news item, or a fearful comment made by someone near me who doesn't understand the power of Jesus' name.

As we begin to take our rightful place of authority with our words and actions, then we become better stewards of any area of life that needs to become more like Jesus: our thoughts, our habits, our health, our food intake, our weight, our emotions, our treatment of others. . . . By keeping our focus on Jesus and the things of God, we go from *"glory to glory"* (2 Corinthians 3:18), we become more like Him and we become better stewards of the gifts God has entrusted to us. (Philippians 2:5)

Can you imagine how this stewardship can allow more of our "light to shine"? And what happens when our light shines? Matthew 5:16 says that others then see our good works, and God is glorified. I'll leave you with 2 more verses: Philippians 4:6, *"Don't worry about anything; instead, pray about everything. Tell God what you need, and thank him for all he has done."* (NLT) And 1 John 4:18, *"Such love has no fear, because perfect love expels all fear. If we are afraid, it is for fear of punishment, and this shows that we have not fully experienced his perfect love."* (NLT) So if you want to be a better steward in <u>every</u> aspect of life, don't give fear any place in your life.

"Paradigm Shifters—Action Points"

1) I've heard it said that fear is having more faith in satan's ability to destroy than in God's ability to restore and protect. What is one thing you fear today that God wants to help you overcome by faith in Him? And remember, faith works by love. (Galatians 5:6) I also like to use 1 John 4:4 and 1 John 4:18 whenever I can: *"Greater is He who is in you than he who is in the world;" "There is no fear in love, but perfect love casts out fear."* (It should go without saying, but it doesn't nowadays, that "perfect love" is not what today's pop singers sing about, what the romance novels describe, or what most actors portray on TV or in movies!)

____

____

____

____

____

2) Jeremiah 29:11 says that God has good plans for our future, not plans for evil or calamity. Why not ask God to show you what His plans are for the next season in your life? Then ask Him how He wants to work through you to make these plans happen. If you let Him, He will show you step by step, for the rest of your time on earth.

____

____

____

____

____

Day 31 Selah-Meditations

(Every now and then I look around and ask myself if satan has been trying to steal something that God wants for me to enjoy, so that I can experience abundant life—not just money, though, by any means.)

John 10:10

The thief cometh not, but for to steal, and to kill, and to destroy: I am come that they might have life, and that they might have it more abundantly. (KJV)

The thief comes only to steal and kill and destroy; I came that they may have life, and have it abundantly. (NASB)

A thief is only there to steal and kill and destroy. I came so they can have real and eternal life, more and better life than they ever dreamed of. (Message)

The thief comes only in order to steal and kill and destroy. I came that they may have and enjoy life, and have it in abundance (to the full, till it overflows). (Amplified)

The thief's purpose is to steal and kill and destroy. My purpose is to give them a rich and satisfying life. (NLT)

The thief comes only to steal and kill and destroy. I came that they may have life and have it abundantly. (ESV)

The thief doth not come, except that he may steal, and kill, and destroy; I came that they may have life, and may have [it] abundantly. (YLT)

A thief comes only to steal and to kill and to destroy. I have come that they may have life and have it in abundance. (HCSB)

The thief comes not but that he may steal, and kill, and destroy: I am come that they might have life, and might have [it] abundantly. (Darby)

A night thief cometh not, but that he steal, slay, and destroy; and I came, that they have life, and have more plenteously. [A night thief cometh not, but that he steal, and slay, and lose; I came, that they have life, and have more plenteously.] (Wycliffe NT)

- Day 32 -

Today's WORD on Money™:
Biblical Profit

But for good stewards, profit should be the fruit or a tool, not the goal.

Have you ever wondered if there is a difference between Biblical profit and worldly profit? And should Christians do the same thing with profit that non-Christians do?

One of the best places to learn what God says about profit is in Matthew 25, the Parable of the Talents. And one of the best teachings that I've seen on this parable is done by my good friend Patrice Tsague (www.nehemiahproject.org). Patrice defines Biblical profit as "the spiritual and natural gains after all costs are deducted from a business transaction or from the revenue of a business."

So far, only the word "spiritual" is substantially different from the world's definition of profit. But what do we do with that profit? There are 3 main things that Christians should do:

1) enhance their product or service; 2) reinvest back into their business to increase production; 3) as Deuteronomy 8:18 says, build wealth so that God establishes His covenant. Establishing this covenant includes numerous things. But as we've mentioned before, God values salvation, discipleship, and service.

We've all seen examples of profits that were used to fund "over the top" lifestyles. Should Christians expect these lifestyles when they profit Biblically? According to Matthew 25 verses 21 and 23, the reward of Biblical profit is not a lavish lifestyle, but more responsibility: *"You have been faithful over a few things, I will make you ruler over many things."* And if I read these verses correctly, this increased responsibility is actually a part of the "joy of the Lord" into which we enter.

So we shouldn't expect to spend all or most of "our" profit on ourselves, even though God loves to bless us with nice things, just as we love to bless <u>our</u> children. We must also realize that as our responsibilities increase, we may need tools that seem lavish or expensive to the uninformed. But for good stewards, profit should be the <u>fruit</u> or a tool, not the goal. The profit is God's because He gave us the talents in the first place. Psalm 35:27 says God takes pleasure in the prosperity of His servants. Since prosperity is not just money, and since we're not the ultimate owners, we should always seek God's counsel first before spending what He has entrusted to us. And although God richly gives us all we need for our enjoyment (1 Timothy 6:17), I know that too often, I've spent God's money like it was mine. The illustration below provides us with some key differences between the 2 types of profit:

BIBLICAL ENTREPRENUER PROFIT

-Has everlasting value
-Is acquired through obedience and proper stewardship
-Is the reward of service
-Is used to build the kingdom of God
-Comes with ultimate fulfillment

WORLDLY PROFIT

-Has limited value
-Is acquired by power and might
-Is the goal
-Is used to feed the lust of the flesh
-Comes with sorrow[1]

In addition to studying what profit is, there is much more to learn about how we should conduct ourselves in the marketplace. I think many of you will be blessed if you learn more about Biblical Entrepreneurship, even if you always plan to be an employee.

[1] From Biblical Entrepreneurship I. For more information, visit www.nehemiahproject.org.

"Paradigm Shifters—Action Points"

1) Think about the events of 2007, 2008 and 2009: the sub-prime scandals, the credit defaults, and more. What can you do within your circle of influence to accomplish the following:

a) Develop the right balance of forgiveness, mercy, and justice
b) Be accountable for your own actions
c) Avoid playing the "blame game"
d) Put your own "house" in order and build it on "solid rock"
e) Influence our leaders to take steps so that these "crises" don't recur.

____

____

____

____

2) 1 Timothy 6:10 (NLT) says this, *"For the love of money is the root of all kinds of evil. And some people, craving money, have wandered from the true faith and pierced themselves with many sorrows."* There are numerous people and companies that we could provide as examples which fulfill this scripture. Instead, let's "own up" to the times when we all have loved money more than God. When we ask God to forgive us, He will. Then we can ask Him to show us how to live in ways that prevent sorrows.

____

____

____

____

Day 32 Selah-Meditations

Habakkuk 2:1-2

I will stand upon my watch, and set me upon the tower, and will watch to see what he will say unto me, and what I shall answer when I am reproved. And the LORD answered me, and said, Write the vision, and make it plain upon tables, that he may run that readeth it. (KJV)

I will stand on my guard post and station myself on the rampart; and I will keep watch to see what He will speak to me, and how I may reply when I am reproved. Then the LORD answered me and said, "Record the vision and inscribe it on tablets, that the one who reads it may run. (NASB)

What's God going to say to my questions? I'm braced for the worst. I'll climb to the lookout tower and scan the horizon. I'll wait to see what God says, how he'll answer my complaint. And then God answered: "Write this. Write what you see. Write it out in big block letters so that it can be read on the run. (Message)

[OH, I know, I have been rash to talk out plainly this way to God!] I will [in my thinking] stand upon my post of observation and station myself on the tower or fortress, and will watch to see what He will say within me and what answer I will make [as His mouthpiece] to the perplexities of my complaint against Him. And the Lord answered me and said, Write the vision and engrave it so plainly upon tablets that everyone who passes may [be able to] read [it easily and quickly] as he hastens by. (Amplified)

I will climb up to my watchtower and stand at my guardpost. There I will wait to see what the Lord says and how he will answer my complaint. Then the Lord said to me, "Write my answer plainly on tablets, so that a runner can carry the correct message to others. (NLT)

I will take my stand at my watchpost and station myself on the tower, and look out to see what he will say to me, and what I will answer concerning my complaint. And the LORD answered me: "Write the vision; make it plain on tablets, so he may run who reads it." (ESV)

On my charge I stand, and I station myself on a bulwark, and I watch to see what He doth speak against me, and what I do reply to my reproof. And Jehovah answereth me and saith: 'Write a vision, and explain on the tables, That he may run who is reading it.' (YLT)

I will stand at my guard post and station myself on the lookout tower. I will watch to see what He will say to me and what I should reply about my complaint. The LORD answered me: Write down this vision; clearly inscribe it on tablets so one may easily read it. (HCSB)

I will stand upon my watch, and set me upon the tower, and will look forth to see what he will say unto me, and what I shall answer as to my reproof. And Jehovah answered me and said, Write the vision, and engrave it upon tablets, that he may run that readeth it. (Darby)

- Day 33 -

Today's WORD on Money™:
Goal Setting for Children of God

. . . I personally should have spent much less time saying*, "God, bless my goal," and more time* asking*, "God, what* is *the goal?"*

Some Christians think that goal setting is unbiblical. For years I too struggled with whether or not I should set goals. Today I'll share why I believe that Christians should be the best goal setters on Planet Earth.

I worked for over 5 years with Success Motivation Institute, an internationally known goal setting and sales training company headquartered here in Waco, Texas. Because I did not know the information that I'm going to share with you in this lesson, I had many bad experiences with goal setting. I set goals, even spiritual goals, but they were my goals, not God's. As a result, I experienced achievement without fulfillment. Not only did I have mixed financial success, but I drifted further away from God in the process.

If I had had a better understanding of Habakkuk chapter 2, I would have had far better results. Verse one says, *"I will climb up to my watchtower and stand at my guardpost. There I will wait to see what the Lord says and how he will answer my complaint."* Now remember, God's Word is like a tapestry, and it is living and active, continually feeding us and helping us grow. Then when we grow, even the same passage can feed us more! But one meaning I take from verse 1 is that I personally should have spent much less time saying, "God, bless *my* goal," and more time asking, "God, what is the goal?" Then I should have waited patiently for His answer.

Instead, I gave lip service to seeking God's face, but then I spent far more time fleshing out "my" plans instead of His. So I encourage all of you to learn from my mistakes. Take far more time to pray and to make sure you have God's wisdom on the directions He has for you. As you do this, I think that you'll often find that the actual planning that He has for you can be accomplished much more quickly and efficiently. You should end up with goals and plans so big that they can't be accomplished without God's help.

Please understand that the planning, and especially the execution of the plans, will still require serious time and effort. But as a pilot, I can tell you from experience that it's much easier to fly with the wind than against the wind. Also note that just as a pilot has to monitor his progress, we too may have to make "course corrections," which may sometimes take the form of correction from God. Also, be willing to be accountable to fellow Christians who can "sharpen your iron."

Habakkuk 2 verse 2 says this: *"Then the Lord said to me, "Write my answer plainly on tablets, so that a runner can carry the correct message to others."* (NLT) From this verse, I understand that Godly goal setting will not only help me to have a good, clear plan of action, but it will also edify and "light the way" for others, perhaps even future generations. So it appears to me that Christians should be the best goal setters and the best goal achievers in the world. If we look to the Bible for examples, we see that God did things through His people that they could never have done without Him. Why would He want anything less for us today?

There are many deep teachings in Habakkuk, more than I can cover in this brief lesson. So I urge you to make a perennial study of this and other passages in the Bible. As you do, I believe you will realize a significant advantage over any method of goal setting that leaves God out of the picture.

"Paradigm Shifters—Action Points"

1) Ask God to show you one of His goals for you. Be quiet and patiently wait, as you learn to discern how He speaks to you. He is hardly ever early, but He's never late. And He is definitely not like a soft drink dispenser where you deposit your money and out pops a drink. You didn't *really* think the Creator of the Universe would operate like that, did you?!

2) Can you remember a time when you couldn't wait for God's answer, so you went ahead on your own, and the results were terrible? I have done that many times. It reminds me of the saying, "If you don't have time to do it right the first time, when are you going to have the time to do it again?" I hope I've gotten the "false starts" out of my system. How about you?

Day 33 Selah-Meditations

(Too many of us in America have forgotten where our wealth came from.)

Deuteronomy 8:18

But thou shalt remember the LORD thy God: for it is he that giveth thee power to get wealth, that he may establish his covenant which he sware unto thy fathers, as it is this day. (KJV)

But you shall remember the LORD your God, for it is He who is giving you power to make wealth, that He may confirm His covenant which He swore to your fathers, as it is this day. (NASB)

Remember that God, your God, gave you the strength to produce all this wealth so as to confirm the covenant that he promised to your ancestors—as it is today. (Message)

But you shall [earnestly] remember the Lord your God, for it is He Who gives you power to get wealth, that He may establish His covenant which He swore to your fathers, as it is this day. (Amplified)

Remember the Lord your God. He is the one who gives you power to be successful, in order to fulfill the covenant he confirmed to your ancestors with an oath. (NLT)

You shall remember the LORD your God, for it is he who gives you power to get wealth, that he may confirm his covenant that he swore to your fathers, as it is this day. (ESV)

And thou hast remembered Jehovah thy God, for He it [is] who is giving to thee power to make wealth, in order to establish His covenant which He hath sworn to thy fathers as [at] this day. (YLT)

but remember that the LORD your God gives you the power to gain wealth, in order to confirm His covenant He swore to your fathers, as it is today. (HCSB)

But thou shalt remember Jehovah thy God, that it is he who giveth thee power to get wealth, that he may establish his covenant which he swore unto thy fathers, as it is this day. (Darby)

- Day 34 -

Today's WORD on Money™: Supernatural Provision or Supernatural Wealth?

"God is not a lottery ticket or a gumball machine!"

Psalm 35:27 says that when we serve God, He takes pleasure in our prosperity. (Prosperity is not limited to financial things.) Hebrews 11:6 says that it is impossible to please God without faith. So if we have faith, does it please God to provide supernatural wealth for us?

If any of you can find an example of instantaneous supernatural wealth creation that we have overlooked, please contact us. But let's begin by looking at some examples of God's supernatural provision for His people. As I think of Job, Abraham, Isaac, Jacob, Joshua, Caleb, Ruth, David, Solomon, Esther, Daniel, and the apostles in the New Testament, I see where God's favor was on their lives. They were very blessed, but in each instance, we read of the work that they did before a breakthrough occurred.

The closest thing to an "overnight" success is probably Joseph's 1-day transition from being a prisoner to being 2nd in command under Pharaoh. But if we look more closely, we see at least 13 years of preparation that took place before Joseph was equipped to step into what God had prepared for him. I don't know of many people who would choose the road to "overnight success" that Joseph had to take! Ruth and Esther also experienced dramatic turnarounds, but there was risk and preparation time involved in their situations as well.

Here are some other examples of supernatural provision. In 1 Kings 17 we read of the widow who fed Elijah with her last resources, and then her oil and flour lasted through the famine. In 2 Kings 4, Elisha instructed the widow to borrow jars and fill them with oil. Then she sold the oil and lived on the remainder. In 2 Kings 6 we read of the borrowed axe head that Elisha made to float so that it could be returned to its owner. And in 2 Kings 7 we read about a city in Samaria that was besieged by the Aramean army. Although 4 lepers and the citizens of the city recovered everything the troops left behind, we don't read that the spoils were enough to sustain the citizens for the rest of their lives.

The pattern that I see in the Bible is that God supernaturally canceled debt and He supernaturally provided for people's needs. But I don't find any instances of where God instantaneously and supernaturally made people so wealthy that they "had it made" for the rest of their lives, without any prior preparation on their part, and without a responsibility to work after the miracle. That says at least 2 things to me about God: 1) as we previously mentioned, God didn't put us here to retire, even when our barns are full; 2) God uses supernatural means to get us out of debt or to provide for a need, but if we are to build wealth, the wealth will be grown over a period of time. This may be because God knows we need a close relationship with Him. Or it may be that He created us because He wants to fellowship with us. Either way, it's pretty clear that God is not an Aladdin's magic lamp that we rub to get riches with no other preparation on our part. One of the best ways I ever heard this described is by someone who said this: "God is not a lottery ticket or a gumball machine!"

Proverbs 21:5 says this, *"Good planning and hard work lead to prosperity, but hasty shortcuts lead to poverty."* (NLT) I'm sure many of you, like me, have been rescued a number of times. It pleases God to prosper us, but in order to build wealth that doesn't evaporate, we'd probably better plan on using a crock pot instead of a microwave! I hope this lesson helps all of you to make good, prosperous plans.

"Paradigm Shifters—Action Points"

1) What kind of habits do you need to acquire or improve upon, to ensure that you don't get ahead of God's plans for you? One of my prayers for years has been, "Father, I want everything You have for me: nothing more, nothing less, and nothing else."

____

____

____

____

____

2) Here are a couple of quick examples to illustrate this week's lesson:

a) Have you ever seen what happens to a butterfly struggling to come out of its cocoon? If you try to help it, it doesn't develop the strength it needs to survive, and it soon dies. The same thing happens if you try to help a baby chick as it pecks its way out of the egg.

b) There are times when true love should say no. I love my daughters, but I would be a poor father to give them automobiles before they have the age and maturity to be competent drivers. No matter how much we whine or squawk, God often graciously protects us from ourselves!

____

____

____

____

____

Day 34 Selah-Meditations

Ecclesiastes 9:10a

Whatsoever thy hand findeth to do, do it with thy might. . . . (KJV)

Whatever your hand finds to do, do it with all your might. . . . (NASB)

Whatever turns up, grab it and do it. And heartily! (Message)

Whatever your hand finds to do, do it with all your might. . . . (Amplified)

Whatever you do, do well. (NLT)

Whatever your hand finds to do, do it with your might. . . . (ESV)

All that thy hand findeth to do, with thy power do. . . . (YLT)

Whatever your hands find to do, do with [all] your strength. . . . (HCSB)

Whatever thy hand findeth to do, do with thy might. . . . (Darby)

- Day 35 -

Today's WORD on Money™:

The Joy of Work!

Christianity . . . holds that we do not have the ability to do enough work to earn our way into heaven . . . .

Do any of you remember the old "Dobie Gillis" show on TV in the early 1960's? I remember Bob Denver, who played a lazy beatnik named Maynard G. Krebs. Denver later played Gilligan on "Gilligan's Island." But any time someone asked Maynard to work, he got really nervous and his voice cracked if he tried to say the word "*work*"! Today we'll compare Maynard's view of work with what the Bible says.

Some people think work is a curse, but it's not. Remember that Adam worked before the fall. The curse just made work more difficult and less productive. But despite that increase in effort and difficulty, work is still meant to be rewarding. And when we listen to God day-by-day, moment-by-moment, our work becomes much more efficient, with much less wasted effort. I've heard that Martin Luther once said that he had so much work to do that day, that the only way he could get it all done was if he spent the first 3 hours of his day in prayer!

So after Adam and Eve left the Garden of Eden, what did God say about work? One thing that God commands many times in the Bible is that we work only 6 days per week. So we shouldn't feel guilty about taking a nap on the Sabbath. I firmly believe that people who don't make it a habit of resting each week are setting themselves up for health problems.

Another thing we discover about work is that it is ubiquitous: God works, good people work, and evil people work. Luke 16 tells us in the Parable of the Unjust Steward that the children of the world are wiser than the children of light. I don't know about you, but I don't like that, so I want to know the Creator of the Universe, and work with His wisdom, not just mine.

As the New Testament mentions work, we see one of the ways in which Christianity differs from other religions. All other major religions require certain works in order for the seekers to qualify for their versions of "eternal life." Christianity, on the other hand, holds that Jesus did the work for us, that we do not have the ability to do enough work to earn our way into heaven, but that all we have to "do" is accept what Jesus did in our place.

We also learn from the Bible that wealth itself can perform work. One of the best examples of this is seen by observing how animals multiply. Abraham became "very rich" in cattle. His livestock multiplied as more and more animals were born and then had offspring of their own. Just like Abraham's livestock, our work produces "fruit" that begins to propagate without our continual direct supervision.

But no matter how hard an investment works on its own, and no matter how hard we work personally, we must remember that God is our source. If we follow His directions, we can have wealth without sorrows. (1 Timothy 6:10) And for those of you who believe you're working where you're called to work, but you want to enjoy your work more, I recommend you read about Brother Lawrence in his book The Practice of the Presence of God. Brother Lawrence was a lay brother in a Carmelite monastery in the 1600's.

"Paradigm Shifters—Action Points"

1) Have you ever not worked hard enough? Have you ever worked too much, or to the detriment of your health or your family? What will you commit to change, in order to achieve a better balance, so that as you increase your faith in God, you let Him handle what you shouldn't?

____

____

____

____

____

____

2) Have you ever tried to assemble something without looking at the instruction manual? I have, but I don't do it anymore. God gave us the Bible to use as an *instruction manual for life*. In spite of what some detractors may say or think, God's Word really will show us the answers we need, or it will point us in the right direction to find those answers.

____

____

____

____

____

____

Day 35 Selah-Meditations

(I love to remind Satan of this verse.)

Proverbs 6:31

But if he be found, he shall restore sevenfold; he shall give all the substance of his house. (KJV)

But when he is found, he must repay sevenfold; He must give all the substance of his house. (NASB)

When he's caught he has to pay it back, even if he has to put his whole house in hock. (Message)

But if he is found out, he must restore seven times [what he stole]; he must give the whole substance of his house [if necessary--to meet his fine]. (Amplified)

But if he is caught, he must pay back seven times what he stole, even if he has to sell everything in his house. (NLT)

but if he is caught, he will pay sevenfold; he will give all the goods of his house. (ESV)

And being found he repayeth sevenfold, All the substance of his house he giveth. (YLT)

Still, if caught, he must pay seven times as much; he must give up all the wealth in his house. (HCSB)

and if he be found, he shall restore sevenfold; he shall give all the substance of his house. (Darby)

- Day 36 -

Today's WORD on Money™:

To Catch a Thief

If you go out on the back porch and want the dog to come to you, then don't call for the cat!

What do you do if something is lost or taken from you? What about if you believe that you're under spiritual attack? Do you go on the defense, on the offense, or do you use both?

Proverbs 6:30-31 says this, *"Excuses might be found for a thief who steals because he is starving. But if he is caught, he must pay back seven times what he stole, even if he has to sell everything in his house."* So here's my question to you: have the devil and his demons ever stolen anything from you? If they have, what does that make them? That's right, they're thieves. So if I feel I've been robbed, I start declaring my sevenfold return. I believe that we can get too expensive for the enemy, so that he and his cohorts "depart for a season".

2 Corinthians says we go from *"glory to glory."* Proverbs 4:8 says that Wisdom will promote us when we exalt it. I heard a preacher say this about promotions: "new level, new devil". We need to be diligent in reminding ourselves who we are in Christ. In fact, that is another study that I would recommend to you: go through the New Testament and study every place where the words "in Christ" or "in Him" are found. You'll probably realize like I did that you have lived well below your privileges, as a child of the King.

So be discerning about your surroundings, your circumstances and the events that are occurring around you. Be quick to recognize a possible attack. Make sure you have your armor on (Ephesians 6:11, and "an ounce of prevention is worth a pound of cure"), and then be bold about using your sword—the Word of God. Remind any attackers that you are in Christ Jesus and He is in you. Since He is the name above all names and everything is under His feet, then the enemy is by definition under your feet also, because you're in Christ.

I also recommend that you have some key scriptures so well memorized that you can quote them at a moment's notice--things like, *"Thanks be to God who always causes us to triumph"* (2 Corinthians 2:14), and *"greater is He that is in me than he that is in the world"* (1 John 4:4). We can't do like Barney Fife and expect the "bad guys" to *wait* until we get our "guns" out (and load the bullets)!

And don't bring rotten circumstances on yourself because of your own careless words. I heard a preacher say it like this, "If you go out on the back porch and want the dog to come to you, then don't call for the cat!" So if you want to be blessed, don't curse yourself. Remember, as you think in your heart, so shall you be (Proverbs 23:7), and *"out of the abundance of the heart, the mouth speaks"* (Matthew 12:34).

Here's another illustration: Philippians 2:5 says we should let the mind be in us which was also in Christ. Do you really think Jesus ever said anything like, "I'm so stupid", or "That just burns me up," or "I'm getting forgetful," or "I'm terrible at names"? If you think that, then I'd recommend you re-read Matthew, Mark, Luke and John a few times! Ephesians 5:1 says that we are to be followers and imitators of Christ. Do that and you'll become increasingly blessed.

"Paradigm Shifters—Action Points"

1) Some people think it's prideful or sacrilegious to say that we are to imitate Christ (Ephesians 5:1). 2 Corinthians 5:21 says that we are the righteousness of God *in Him* (italics added). Without God's help we are powerless. Psalm 37:4 says that if we will delight ourselves in the Lord, then He will give us the desires of our hearts. I see this promise working from both directions: on the one hand, as we learn God's ways of doing and being right, then we no longer desire many of the things we formerly did. On the other hand, God loves to bless us, as long as He knows that what He gives us won't cause us to forget that He is our source.

____

____

____

____

____

2) If you're like me regarding your past, you may want to re-visit some of your previous desires, dreams, and failures. Not only will you develop more understanding of how you can improve, but you may even find something that you can resurrect, now that you have a better idea of why it failed. Then again, you may look at other things and no longer want them, because you now realize that <u>God alone</u> is and has something so much better for you! Many times I have later thanked God for answering my prayers with a "no"!

____

____

____

____

____

Day 36 Selah-Meditations

Because of tomorrow's topic, we're providing one translation of an entire chapter. This weekend's meditation is Psalm 139. Consider memorizing verses 13-15, or 1 Timothy 6:6-9.

1 O Lord, you have examined my heart
and know everything about me.
2 You know when I sit down or stand up.
You know my thoughts even when I'm far away.
3 You see me when I travel
and when I rest at home.
You know everything I do.
4 You know what I am going to say
even before I say it, Lord.
5 You go before me and follow me.
You place your hand of blessing on my head.
6 Such knowledge is too wonderful for me,
too great for me to understand!
7 I can never escape from your Spirit!
I can never get away from your presence!
8 If I go up to heaven, you are there;
if I go down to the grave, you are there.
9 If I ride the wings of the morning,
if I dwell by the farthest oceans,
10 even there your hand will guide me,
and your strength will support me.
11 I could ask the darkness to hide me
and the light around me to become night—
12 but even in darkness I cannot hide from you.
To you the night shines as bright as day.
Darkness and light are the same to you.
13 You made all the delicate, inner parts of my body
and knit me together in my mother's womb.
14 Thank you for making me so wonderfully complex!
Your workmanship is marvelous—how well I know it.
15 You watched me as I was being formed in utter seclusion,
as I was woven together in the dark of the womb.
16 You saw me before I was born.
Every day of my life was recorded in your book.
Every moment was laid out before a single day had passed.

17 How precious are your thoughts about me, O God.
They cannot be numbered!
18 I can't even count them;
they outnumber the grains of sand!
And when I wake up,
you are still with me!
19 O God, if only you would destroy the wicked!
Get out of my life, you murderers!
20 They blaspheme you;
your enemies misuse your name.
21 O Lord, shouldn't I hate those who hate you?
Shouldn't I despise those who oppose you?
22 Yes, I hate them with total hatred,
for your enemies are my enemies.
23 Search me, O God, and know my heart;
test me and know my anxious thoughts.
24 Point out anything in me that offends you,
and lead me along the path of everlasting life. (NLT)

1Timothy 6:6-9

But godliness with contentment is a great gain. For we brought nothing into the world, and we can take nothing out. But if we have food and clothing, we will be content with these. But those who want to be rich fall into temptation, a trap, and many foolish and harmful desires, which plunge people into ruin and destruction. (HCSB)

But godliness actually is a means of great gain when accompanied by contentment. For we have brought nothing into the world, so we cannot take anything out of it either. If we have food and covering, with these we shall be content. But those who want to get rich fall into temptation and a snare and many foolish and harmful desires which plunge men into ruin and destruction. (NASB)

A devout life does bring wealth, but it's the rich simplicity of being yourself before God. Since we entered the world penniless and will leave it penniless, if we have bread on the table and shoes on our feet, that's enough. But if it's only money these leaders are after, they'll self-destruct in no time. Lust for money brings trouble and nothing but trouble. (Message)

Yet true godliness with contentment is itself great wealth. After all, we brought nothing with us when we came into the world, and we can't take anything with us when we leave it. So if we have enough food and clothing, let us be content. But people who long to be rich fall into temptation and are trapped by many foolish and harmful desires that plunge them into ruin and destruction. (NLT)

- Day 37 -

Today's WORD on Money™: Politically or Spiritually Correct?

. . . the "Evidence Bible" reminds us that without Jesus we are damned, regardless of our sexual preferences (www.livingwaters.com).

No matter which political party is in power, there are several core beliefs that Christians should continue to remind our leaders to embrace, based upon God's Word, and upon the rights we have in America to require our leaders to represent us.

Much of this lesson was taken from my pastor's sermon, delivered on November 2, 2008[1]. No matter what the political issue-du-jour, the Bible contains principles that will give us the wisdom to know what stand we should take. I will limit our lesson to 4 key issues, even though the Bible has answers for any issue that will ever be debated.

First, what does God say about the **ECONOMY**? As Christians, we should not point fingers at either the Left or the Right. The economic problems that surfaced in 2008 are due to greed, both corporate and personal greed, including yours and mine. The policies of Wall Street, Main Street and Capitol Hill have all failed many times. At all levels, beginning with you and me, Americans need to repent and do 3 key things: live simply, work diligently, and give generously. Study 1st Timothy 6:6-9 on the previous page.

Second, what does God say about the **POOR**? As Christians, we should be merciful, actively helping the poor, not only giving them a fish, but teaching them to fish, as well. If we abdicate our responsibility to do so, then government will increase our taxes and do an inferior job of what the Church should be doing. On Day 18 and in other lessons, I share examples of what our family does to minister to the poor. Ask God how He wants you and your family to serve.

Third, what does God say about **MARRIAGE**? God communicates to us through the family. The family is the building block, the foundation of our society. Satan knows if he can destroy a nation's families, he can destroy that country. Sadly, Christian families in America have been broken as much as non-Christian families. Defining marriage is not a political issue, it's a spiritual issue. God made males and females for a purpose. Two sperm cannot create life, nor can 2 eggs create life. Only a sperm and an egg can join together and "become as one." Trying politically to change the definition of marriage can never address the spiritual, or even the biological roots of the issue. Homosexual marriage is a non sequitur. But it does not follow that Christians should abandon civility. God alone is the ultimate judge. He doesn't love everything people do, but He loved every person on this planet enough to send His Son to die for us. He loves people so much that He won't force us to go to Heaven. We can choose Hell if we want. It breaks His heart when people make that choice, but while we're on earth, He won't "make" us do something against our will. More to the point, the "Evidence Bible" reminds us that without Jesus we are damned, regardless of our sexual preferences (www.livingwaters.com).

Fourth, what does God say about **LIFE**? God loves you and me; He tells us that life and death, blessing and cursing are set before us and that therefore we should Choose Life. God is For Us and FOR LIFE, so He is "Pro" Life! If someone doubts this, look first at a sonogram. If that doesn't convince you, visit the neonatal intensive care unit (NICU) at your local hospital. Look at a premature baby: watch her breathe, watch her heart beat and her fingers move, and then tell me that is not life. Again, this is a spiritual issue, not a politically correct or incorrect issue. I encourage you to study what God's Word says on these and other issues. Then exercise your freedom of speech and hold your elected officials' feet to the fire. If their records don't line up with God's Word, then vote them out of office.

[1] For an mp3 of the sermon, visit www.antiochcc.net. For more about our pastor, Jimmy Seibert, please read his book, The Church Can Change the World.

"Paradigm Shifters—Action Points"

1) I encourage all of you, regardless of your political affiliations, and regardless of who is in office, to pray for our leaders. Pray for both appointed and elected officials at all levels: local, district, state, regional, and federal/national. Proverbs 21:1 tells us that the king's heart is in God's hand, and that God can turn it however and wherever He wants.

____

____

____

____

____

2) What can you do in love to magnify God's views on political issues?

____

____

____

____

____

____

Day 37 Selah-Meditations

(See also 2 Corinthians 9:6.)

Proverbs 11:24

But this [is true], he that sows sparingly shall reap also sparingly; and he that sows in [the spirit of] blessing shall reap also in blessing: (KJV)

There is one who scatters, and yet increases all the more, and there is one who withholds what is justly due, and yet it results only in want. (NASB)

The world of the generous gets larger and larger; the world of the stingy gets smaller and smaller. (Message)

There are those who [generously] scatter abroad, and yet increase more; there are those who withhold more than is fitting or what is justly due, but it results only in want. (Amplified)

Give freely and become more wealthy; be stingy and lose everything. (NLT)

One gives freely, yet grows all the richer; another withholds what he should give, and only suffers want. (ESV)

There is who is scattering, and yet is increased, and who is keeping back from uprightness, only to want. (YLT)

One person gives freely, yet gains more; another withholds what is right, only to become poor. (HCSB)

There is that scattereth, and yet increaseth; and there is that withholdeth more than is right, but [it tendeth] only to want. (Darby)

- Day 38 -

Today's WORD on Money™: How Do We Treat People?

Ray Lyne says that he can tell about people's love for God and their true commitment to helping the poor by how they tip the housekeepers.

Over the past few years, reality TV shows have become very popular. Today I'll give a few real-life examples of how putting our faith into action can make a difference in our daily lives, and in the lives of others. I think these differences are much more valuable than winning a TV show prize.

We spoke earlier of our family's garage "giveaways." That is one example of something we have done to help the poor. We also formed a non-profit corporation as a giving vehicle. You don't have to incorporate, though, so give whether or not God directs you to form a corporation.

When our family travels, we usually take some of our favorite spiritual books and DVD's with us. We enjoy meeting people in different places and striking up conversations with them. For example, we usually pray in restaurants, so when we do, we ask the waiter or waitress if there is anything that we could pray about for them or their family. We have had waitresses break down and cry at this request. Many of us are far too insensitive to the needs of others. We have found that many of those who hold lower paying jobs feel overlooked and taken for granted. Many have been overjoyed and incredulous when they realized that one of their customers actually cared enough to ask about them.

One note of caution here: don't offer to pray for a waiter and then leave a stingy tip! I've heard that many waiters and waitresses believe that Christians eating out for lunch on Sundays are some of the most difficult customers to please. Let's go out and erase that stereotype! Treat them with love and be generous with your tips.

Here's another example. When my wife and I are getting technical support or customer service on the phone, we often ask the personnel if we could pray for them or their family. We've almost never had someone who did not appreciate these requests, and we've even corresponded repeatedly with some of these people. I've even gotten to know some Dell employees personally. I've stayed in touch with one young man, taken him to lunch when I was visiting his city, and sent gifts when he and his wife had a new baby. I don't say this to brag, but to encourage you to examine how you may have overlooked opportunities to share God's love with others.

Checkout stands present another opportunity for us to show the people who ring up our purchases that someone cares about them. Many are surprised and pleased when we call them by name. Our family also enjoys blessing hotel housekeepers. We have met some of the sweetest people "behind the scenes." They are so appreciative when we give them a DVD and money for their family. *Ray Lyne says that he can tell about people's love for God and their true commitment to helping the poor by* how they tip the housekeepers. So be a blessing to a hurting world.

Luke 12:21 encourages us to be rich toward God. Matthew 25 says that when we bless "the least of these," we bless God. There are many ways besides preaching to let people know that God loves them. I can tell you from personal experience that Proverbs 11:24 is real. We have scattered yet God has increased us. On the other hand I know of people who were stingy, and yet their net worth decreased. These are just a few of the ways that almost all of us can share "salt, light, and living water" with those around us.

"Paradigm Shifters—Action Points"

1) Pick one way to be a blessing this week, either somewhere you frequent, or to someone you have previously overlooked.

____

____

____

____

____

____

2) Some people think that the only way you can tell someone about God is to get in their face, or preach on the street corner. And some people do respond well to those approaches. But God gave each of us a unique set of gifts. Use the things you enjoy. For example, I've been in sales since I was 12 years old, so asking questions comes naturally to me. If I'm in a store and someone says something that indicates to me that they may not be very aware of the things of God, I ask God to give me something to ask or say that will cause them to think. Sometimes the conversation develops into a great discussion, and sometimes it doesn't. For me, it's like fishing: you toss something out there and if the time and place are right, you'll get some interest. How does God want to shine through you? [1]

____

____

____

____

[1] For more information on how you can "shine," especially in business, read Kris Den Besten's book, Shine.

Day 38 Selah-Meditations

(If we lived in the early 1800's and bought someone, what would we call that person? A slave, right? That's what the Apostle Paul called himself—God's slave. God bought us. He calls us His children, but since He owns us, shouldn't we do everything we can to live like we're His?)

1 Corinthians 6:20

For ye are bought with a price: therefore glorify God in your body, and in your spirit, which are God's. (KJV)

For you have been bought with a price: therefore glorify God in your body. (NASB)

God owns the whole works. So let people see God in and through your body. (Message)

You were bought with a price [purchased with a preciousness and paid for, made His own]. So then, honor God and bring glory to Him in your body. (Amplified)

for God bought you with a high price. So you must honor God with your body. (NLT)

for you were bought with a price. So glorify God in your body. (ESV)

for ye were bought with a price; glorify, then, God in your body and in your spirit, which are God's. (YLT)

for you were bought at a price; therefore glorify God in your body. (HCSB)

for ye have been bought with a price: glorify now then God in your body. (Darby)

For ye be bought with great price. Glorify ye, and bear ye God in your body. (Wycliffe NT)

- Day 39 -

Today's WORD on Money™: Spiritual, Then Mechanical

For Christians, giving money is first a spiritual process, and then it's a mechanical process.

Most people have heard the scripture that says the love of money is the root of all evil. Some people have over-reacted by deciding to earn as little money as possible. Today we're going to discuss some of the spiritual aspects of money.

I believe that one of the reasons that the Bible has over 2000 scriptures that deal with money and wealth is because money has many God-like qualities. It can bring protection, comfort and security. It can be reassuring. It can even buy peace, for a time. Of course what money buys is a cheap imitation of what God wants to provide. For example, the peace that money buys is very temporary at best. Just look at the lives of some of the wealthy people in Hollywood. If they have peace, why have they been married 4 times? Why do they get hooked on drugs?

French mathematician-philosopher Blaise Pascal said that inside each of us there is a God-shaped hole that can only be filled by a relationship with God. Money won't fill it. Sex won't fill it. Fame, power, business success, and sports championships won't fill it either. Most of us have tried some of these other things, but the satisfaction they bring is fleeting. I myself tried to satisfy my hunger for God with other things, so I know from experience that everything besides God is a distant 2nd place.

But here's the paradox: once we truly make Jesus the Lord of our lives, He doesn't mind it if we enjoy life! In fact, He ardently wants us to enjoy life (John 10:10). And, again from personal experience, life is so much more enjoyable without a hangover!! So for those of you who want to improve your financial results by doing things God's way, let me share with you a couple of the pointers I have learned. I'm not an expert by any means, but I have had a few "learning experiences" that may be helpful.

For non-Christians, giving money away is a mechanical process. For Christians, giving money is first a spiritual process, and then it's a mechanical process. (See Matthew 16:26-ff. for further study.) But giving isn't the only financial process that is spiritual. Once we believe that God is the Owner of all, and we commit to making all of our financial decisions based upon what we believe He wants us to do, then all of our financial activity is spiritual. That means that earning money is a spiritual process, spending money is a spiritual process, and saving and investing money are spiritual processes.

Here's another "outside the box" idea: once you acknowledge that it's better to lay up treasures in Heaven than on earth, then in addition to "retirement" or "redirection" planning, you can do "reward planning."

For example, whether or not Billy Graham is a financial millionaire, by almost anyone's measure, he is a "souls multi-millionaire." There are millions of people who became Christians because of hearing him preach. That's quite a reward Dr. Graham can expect! How about you—how much treasure do you have in Heaven?

"Paradigm Shifters—Action Points"

1) Are you using money (or other "idols") anywhere in your life as a substitute for God's best? Ask God to show you, and when He does, ask Him to help you make a "180."

____

____

____

____

____

____

2) What's one thing you can do this week to make a deposit in your "rewards account"? Some people either complain about or make fun of Christians who tell others about Jesus. But really, if you think about it, it's just human nature to share. If I eat at a good restaurant, read a good book, or see a great movie, I'm not going to keep quiet about it. Why should Christians allow themselves to be denigrated for wanting to share, especially since one's eternal destination is the ultimate "big decision"?

____

____

____

____

____

____

Day 39 Selah-Meditations

(Who are you "hanging out" with?)

Psalm 1:1

Blessed is the man that walketh not in the counsel of the ungodly, nor standeth in the way of sinners, nor sitteth in the seat of the scornful. (KJV)

How blessed is the man who does not walk in the counsel of the wicked, nor stand in the path of sinners, nor sit in the seat of scoffers! (NASB)

How well God must like you— you don't hang out at Sin Saloon, you don't slink along Dead-End Road, you don't go to Smart-Mouth College. (Message)

BLESSED (HAPPY, fortunate, prosperous, and enviable) is the man who walks and lives not in the counsel of the ungodly [following their advice, their plans and purposes], nor stands [submissive and inactive] in the path where sinners walk, nor sits down [to relax and rest] where the scornful [and the mockers] gather. (Amplified)

Oh, the joys of those who do not follow the advice of the wicked, or stand around with sinners, or join in with mockers. (NLT)

Blessed is the man who walks not in the counsel of the wicked, nor stands in the way of sinners, nor sits in the seat of scoffers; (ESV)

O the happiness of that one, who Hath not walked in the counsel of the wicked. And in the way of sinners hath not stood, and in the seat of scorners hath not sat; (YLT)

How happy is the man who does not follow the advice of the wicked, or take the path of sinners, or join a group of mockers! (HCSB)

Blessed is the man that walketh not in the counsel of the wicked, and standeth not in the way of sinners, and sitteth not in the seat of scorners; (Darby)

Day 40

Today's WORD on Money™: How to Find a Biblical Advisor

As we conclude our 40 day study of what "God's Instruction Manual" says about financial issues, I know some of you are probably looking for someone to advise you on how to act on some of the concepts that we've shared. Today we'll share some advice that we hope will help you to find the right financial advisor.

There are two organizations that I can recommend, whose members might be able to advise you. I belong to both of these organizations, and there are some quality people in both groups. No organization is perfect though, and by no means do I know every member. So I'll give you a few questions that you can ask someone, if it's not practical for you to work with our firm. After contacting people in these organizations, if you still do not find someone with whom you are comfortable, contact us and we'll try to put you in touch with someone.

The first organization that I joined, soon after it began, is the National Association of Christian Financial Consultants. They have been around since the late 1990's. Their website is www.nacfc.org. The second organization that I joined has been around since 2003. Their President is Ron Blue, of whom many of you have heard. Their website is www.kingdomadvisors.org. Kingdom Advisors is a larger organization than NACFC. NACFC's members are all in the financial services profession. KA's members can be attorneys, CPA's or other types of financial professionals, as well as financial advisors. Both groups have wonderful annual conferences, so if any of you are in financial services and were not aware of these 2 groups, I urge you to join!

Once you've found someone in your area, here are some of the questions I think you should ask:

1) How long have you been an advisor?
2) What are the strengths and weaknesses of your firm?
3) Do you offer alternative investments in addition to traditional stocks, bonds and insurance?
4) Do you offer the "Infinite Banking" insurance strategy? How long have you offered it?
5) Tell me about your Broker-Dealer/Back Office Support--do they support <u>Biblical</u> Investing?
6) Do you have a minimum account size or a minimum annual fee?
7) How do you help your clients invest Biblically? (They should be able to give you specific products and strategies that they use, and others that they avoid.)
8) What is a profile of your typical client? What is your *ideal* client's profile?
9) How do you service your clients? (Do they have regular face-to-face meetings, online account access, workshops, annual reviews, phone calls, emails, etc.? Few firms will offer all of these services, so you can base your decision in part by how you like information presented. This will help you know which advisors "speak your language."
10) How do you get paid? (There are 3 ways: fee-based, fee only, and commission, each with its own advantages and disadvantages. Some advisors do a combination of fees and commissions.)

There are many other questions you could ask, but these are a good start.

I hope this book has helped you, and I hope you've enjoyed the lessons as much as I enjoyed presenting them. Please contact us if we can serve you, and please let us know if you have investment or product questions you'd like us to answer in our next book, which we hope to publish in 2011.

May each and every one of you experience God's best in every area of your life!

"Paradigm Shifters—Action Points"

1) If you haven't made any changes in your financial situation yet, why not? What can you do TODAY to take a first step to improve upon your current situation? Do you need to call an advisor? Do you need to start a savings plan? Do you want more life insurance? If your list is long, don't be overwhelmed, just pick the most urgent or important matter and take at least one action today!

____

____

____

____

____

____

2) I started thinking about this book about 2 years ago. I knew one thing that would help me get started was to tell others that I planned to write a book. I told some people whom I knew would "bug" me and hold me accountable until I completed it.

In the course of these last 2 years, many other people have told me that they wanted to write a book, but that they haven't done so yet. I made the writing of this book so important that I could not imagine not finishing it. In addition, I believed so strongly that many people are hungering for this type of information, so if I went for a time without writing, I would sternly challenge myself, because I earnestly believed that laziness would deprive someone of life-changing information. That may sound egotistical, but it's not, because everything good that I have, in this book or otherwise, is due to the grace of God. So I encourage you to do whatever it takes (as long as it's legal, moral and ethical) to do what you believe is God's purpose for you.

Day 40 Selah-Meditations

2 Corinthians 5:17

Therefore if any man be in Christ, he is a new creature: old things are passed away; behold, all things are become new. (KJV)

Therefore if anyone is in Christ, he is a new creature; the old things passed away; behold, new things have come. (NASB)

Now we look inside, and what we see is that anyone united with the Messiah gets a fresh start, is created new. The old life is gone; a new life burgeons! Look at it! (Message)

Therefore if any person is [ingrafted] in Christ (the Messiah) he is a new creation (a new creature altogether); the old [previous moral and spiritual condition] has passed away. Behold, the fresh and new has come! (Amplified)

This means that anyone who belongs to Christ has become a new person. The old life is gone; a new life has begun! (NLT)

Therefore, if anyone is in Christ, he is a new creation. The old has passed away; behold, the new has come. (ESV)

so that if any one [is] in Christ -- [he is] a new creature; the old things did pass away, lo, become new have the all things. (YLT)

Therefore if anyone is in Christ, there is a new creation; old things have passed away, and look, new things have come. (HCSB)

So if any one [be] in Christ, [there is] a new creation; the old things have passed away; behold all things have become new: (Darby)

Therefore if any new creature is in Christ, the old things be passed [old things have passed]. Lo! All things be made new, (Wycliffe NT)

Holiday-Bonus Materials

New Year's Day

Today's WORD on Money™:

Your Best Year Yet!

As my friend Dan Stratton says, may this year be your best year yet. Not your best year ever, but your best year yet!

Today you may be watching parades or football games, thinking about a new exercise program, or enjoying time with family and friends. I encourage you to spend some time today asking yourself two things. Then write your answers down and put them into action every day this year.

1) What can I improve this year to bring more glory to God and to walk in more of the good things that God has planned for me? (Ephesians 2:10, Jeremiah 29:11)

2) What habits or behaviors should I get rid of this year, so that I go from "glory to glory" and so that I don't cause someone else to sin?

I know--these are tough questions. But I think you'll agree that if you take the time today, and maybe even for the week, to do some soul searching, then this year could be your best year yet.

Let me share with you a few thought-provoking questions to get you started.

1) Should you eat or drink more of something and less or none of something else? (I recently read of a study which showed that

simply eliminating soft drinks, even diet sodas, was one of the top 4 predictors of longevity in women!) For this question and the next two, my pastor has a great quote: "Christians should not have evangelical minds and pagan bodies."

2) Do you dress appropriately? Is your attire modest, or have you bought into Hollywood's lies? (It amazes me sometimes when even Christian women want men to respect them for their minds, and then they expose massive amounts of their bodies! Christian women, please don't cause your Christian brothers to stumble! Seek God's approval, not the approval of people.)

3) Men, ask yourselves this: are you avoiding everything that can cause you to stumble sexually? If pornography is a temptation, have you installed whatever you need on your computer to block what you shouldn't view? If not, get rid of your computer, don't stay at hotels with black boxes, get accountability partners, or do whatever it takes! My good friend Terry Ermoian has a ministry that can help. Go to www.settingcaptivesfree.com. Terry tells me that since our culture is so loose morally, it's hard for men to avoid the first look at an improperly dressed woman. But a committed Christian then quickly looks away and doesn't look a second time. God help us!

4) Do you invest in companies that profit from or support activities which are not in concert with your moral and Biblical values? (A Biblical advisor will have access to information that can help you answer that question.)

5) If you're married, do you pray with your spouse? I recently heard that Christian couples experience about the same divorce rate as non-Christian couples, approximately 50%. But for Christian couples who pray together, only 1 in 1000 get divorced!

If those 5 questions don't fire you up, then your wood is wet! As my friend Dan Stratton says, may this year be your best year yet. Not your best year ever, but your best year yet!

Scripture--Mark 12:29-31

And Jesus answered him, The first of all the commandments is, Hear, O Israel; The Lord our God is one Lord: And thou shalt love the Lord thy God with all thy heart, and with all thy soul, and with all thy mind, and with all thy strength: this is the first commandment. And the second is like, namely this, Thou shalt love thy neighbour as thyself. There is none other commandment greater than these. (KJV)

Jesus answered, "The foremost is, 'HEAR, O ISRAEL! THE LORD OUR GOD IS ONE LORD; AND YOU SHALL LOVE THE LORD YOUR GOD WITH ALL YOUR HEART, AND WITH ALL YOUR SOUL, AND WITH ALL YOUR MIND, AND WITH ALL YOUR STRENGTH.' "The second is this, 'YOU SHALL LOVE YOUR NEIGHBOR AS YOURSELF.' There is no other commandment greater than these." (NASB)

Jesus said, "The first in importance is, 'Listen, Israel: The Lord your God is one; so love the Lord God with all your passion and prayer and intelligence and energy.' And here is the second: 'Love others as well as you love yourself.' There is no other commandment that ranks with these." (Message)

Jesus answered, The first and principal one of all commands is: Hear, O Israel, The Lord our God is one Lord; And you shall love the Lord your God out of and with your whole heart and out of and with all your soul (your life) and out of and with all your mind (with your faculty of thought and your moral understanding) and out of and with all your strength. This is the first and principal commandment. The second is like it and is this, You shall love your neighbor as yourself. There is no other commandment greater than these. (Amplified)

Jesus replied, "The most important commandment is this: 'Listen, O Israel! The Lord our God is the one and only Lord. And you must love the Lord your God with all your heart, all your soul, all your mind, and all your strength.' The second is equally important: 'Love your neighbor as yourself.' No other commandment is greater than these." (NLT)

Jesus answered, "The most important is, 'Hear, O Israel: The Lord our God, the Lord is one. And you shall love the Lord your God with all your heart and with all your soul and with all your mind and with all your strength.' The second is this: 'You shall love your neighbor as yourself.' There is no other commandment greater than these." (ESV)

and Jesus answered him -- `The first of all the commands [is], Hear, O Israel, the Lord is our God, the Lord is one; and thou shalt love the Lord thy God out of all thy heart, and out of thy soul, and out of all thine understanding, and out of all thy strength -- this [is] the first command; and the second [is] like [it], this, Thou shalt love thy neighbor as thyself; -- greater than these there is no other command.' (YLT)

"This is the most important," Jesus answered: Listen, Israel! The Lord our God, The Lord is One. Love the Lord your God with all your heart, with all your soul, with all your mind, and with all your strength. "The second is: Love your neighbor as yourself. There is no other commandment greater than these." (HCSB)

And Jesus answered him, [The] first commandment of all [is], Hear, Israel: the Lord our God is one Lord; and thou shalt love the Lord thy God with all thy heart, and with all thy soul, and with all thine understanding, and with all thy strength. This is [the] first commandment. And a second like it [is] this: Thou shalt love thy neighbour as thyself. There is not another commandment greater than these. (Darby)

And Jesus answered to him, That the first commandment of all is, Hear thou, Israel, thy Lord God is one God; and thou shalt love thy Lord God of all thine heart, and of all thy soul, and of all thy mind, and of all thy might [and thou shalt love the Lord thy God of all thine heart, and of all thy soul, and of all thy mind, and of all thy virtue, *or strength*]. This is the first commandment. And the second is like to this, Thou shalt love thy neighbour as thyself. There is none other commandment greater than these. (Wycliffe NT)

MLK Birthday
Today's WORD on Money™:
"The Content of Their Character"

. . . it is my prayer that Christ-followers will more fully manifest the lifestyle differences which reflect a truly renewed inner character that can only result from knowing Jesus.

During the Presidential Campaign back in 2000, it dawned on me how much American moral standards have changed since the 1960's. On August 28, 1963, Martin Luther King, whose birthday we celebrate today, stood on the steps of the Lincoln Memorial and said, among other things, that he had a dream that someday his children would be judged not by the color of their skin, but by the "content of their character."

By the fall of 2000, Al Gore, trying to distance himself from President Clinton, said he didn't want to discuss character, but he instead wanted to focus on "issues." Like Dr. King, I believe that character is the issue. Let me hasten to add that Mr. Gore's position on character is not unique to Democrats! But let's look at what a Christian view of character should look like. My good friend and mentor Patrice Tsague, who was born in Cameroon, Africa, and whose mother still serves in that country's government, discusses character in Biblical Entrepreneurship I. [1]

Brother Patrice shares from Acts 6:3 the character traits that the Apostles wanted in the men who would serve as deacons to the early church. Patrice defines character as "The combination of spiritual, moral and ethical qualities that publicly distinguish a person, i.e., reputation." Integrity is "The state of completeness; how (people) behave or the choices they make when no one is watching." Being full of wisdom is "The ability given by God to use good judgment and to act according to the knowledge and understanding of God's word."

A few weeks before the election in 2000, I sent a letter to the editor of the Waco paper. It wasn't printed. Basically it was a tongue-in-cheek letter, urging voters to join the new political party that I said I wanted to start. The name of this fictional party was the C.R.A.S.H. party: **C**itizens' **R**ights on **A**ll **S**treets and **H**ighways. I said that no one had the right to make me drive only on the right hand side of the road. I should be able to drive on both sides whenever I wanted!

To me, this is the type of argument that I hear people making when they want more "rights," whether it be gay rights or many other rights. In other words, even if it kills them, they believe that they should have the right to live however they want. As I said in a previous lesson, although I am saddened by their choices, I defend their right to make them. But I should not be obligated to "pick up the pieces" which result from their poor choices with the health insurance premiums or the tax dollars that I pay. I will pray for them, and I will exercise my freedom of speech to point out my beliefs, but in the end, I believe they should be allowed to choose life or choose death. But I think that the way smokers are treated provides a good model for how we should treat those who make other poor health choices. Those who make good choices in the areas of exercise, diet, and Biblical monogamy, for example, should receive such incentives as premium insurance ratings and prime health care coverage at reduced prices.

Thus, it is my prayer that Christ-followers will more fully manifest the lifestyle differences which reflect a truly renewed inner character that can only result from knowing Jesus (2 Corinthians 2:14). Then, more people will not deceived by any lie that promises the kind of joy that only Jesus can give.

[1] I highly recommend BE 1, 2, and 3 for anyone who wants to start or grow a business God's way. For more information, contact us, or visit www.nehemiahproject.org.

Valentine's Day
Today's WORD on Money™:
Communicating with Your Spouse about Money

What wife would not love to have a husband like the one described in Ephesians 5:25?

Money and finances are said to be the #1 topic of argument in many Christian marriages. Money is most often cited as the biggest factor causing divorce. Jesus said in Matthew 19 that humans should not separate what God has united. Now for those of you who have experienced divorce, this lesson is not meant to condemn you. But it is my prayer that this information will help all of you to have a more Godly marriage from now on.

In the past, our firm has done workshops and retreats to help couples understand how each spouse views money. For example, some people have a scarcity mentality, others have an affluence mentality. Some see money as status, others see it as security. Also, many couples don't understand how to communicate in words that their spouse understands. One spouse may be very abstract and the other very concrete, for instance. (Yes, Virginia, opposites do attract. . . .)

Then there are even various issues within the larger topic of money: maybe the couple's cash flow is fine, but they plan poorly for their tax payments. Or maybe they have done a good job at staying out of debt, but they haven't made provisions for their children's education costs.

I think now you may see that there can be so many variables involved in these issues, that communication can be very difficult. At this point, couples must remember Ephesians 4:15 and "*speak the truth in love*" to each other.

Martin Luther said, "***Let the wife make the husband glad to come home, and let the husband make the wife sorry to see him leave***."

What wife would not love to have a husband like the one described in Ephesians 5:25? [1] God created men and women to be equal. To the extent women have not been treated equally, I agree with the Women's Movement. But men, if we would step up and love women like Christ loved the church, I think we would remove most of the fuel that fires radical women's rights groups today. For that matter, our demonstrating true Christian love would remove the fuel from many other "rights" groups also.

I pray that today each of us will redouble our commitment to love and honor our spouse.

[1] "*For husbands, this means love your wives, just as Christ loved the church.* He gave up his life *for her to make her holy and clean, washed by the cleansing of God's word.*" (Ephesians 5:26-27, NLT) (underline added)

Presidents' Day
Today's WORD on Money™:
"Will" versus "Shall"

. . . it's important for us all to remember how important truth and integrity were to our Founding Fathers.

As we honor our Presidents and even our Founding Fathers today, let's remember some of the beliefs and principles that made many of them so special.

Whenever possible, our firm tries to recommend other Christian financial professionals to help us serve the clients with whom we work. Kurtis Ward, a Christian attorney from Oklahoma once told me a true story to illustrate the difference between the words "shall" and "will." A businessman once related to Kurtis a strange business transaction that the businessman had with a new client. He said that the client went through one of the businessman's contracts and everywhere a certain word occurred, the new client scratched it out and replaced it with another word. The businessman said that he thought the client was not very bright. Kurtis said, "I think I know what the two words were." The businessman was surprised when Kurtis asked, "Was the first word 'will' and the second word 'shall'? He asked Kurtis how he knew.

Kurtis said something to the effect that the word "will" leaves some "wiggle room," but the word "shall" doesn't. To that, the businessman replied something like, "Wow, I guess he wasn't so dumb after all."

On President's Day, as we honor the leaders of our country, I believe that it's important for us all to remember how important truth and integrity were to our Founding Fathers. Their words meant something, and they didn't try to "wiggle" out of their commitments. And where did most of our Founding Fathers acquire their values? Despite what some revisionists would like us to believe, most of our Founding Fathers were staunch Christians. My prayer is that America would realize that our problems ultimately stem from spiritual issues, and that we would heed 2 Chronicles 7:14 and turn back to God.

So for those of you who enjoy word studies and historical information, spend some time reading our country's founding documents. It's also fascinating to research all of God's promises in the Bible which use the word "shall."

One of the best collections of information on our country's Christian heritage can be obtained at www.wallbuilders.org. David Barton has done exhaustive studies on our nation's truly Christian foundations. I highly commend his work to you.

Scripture--2 Chronicles 16:9

For the eyes of the LORD run to and fro throughout the whole earth, to shew himself strong in the behalf of them whose heart is perfect toward him. (KJV)

"For the eyes of the LORD move to and fro throughout the earth that He may strongly support those whose heart is completely His." (NASB)

God is always on the alert, constantly on the lookout for people who are totally committed to him. (Message)

For the eyes of the Lord run to and fro throughout the whole earth to show Himself strong in behalf of those whose hearts are blameless toward Him. (Amplified)

The eyes of the Lord search the whole earth in order to strengthen those whose hearts are fully committed to him. (NLT)

For the eyes of the LORD run to and fro throughout the whole earth, to give strong support to those whose heart is blameless toward him. (ESV)

for Jehovah -- His eyes go to and fro in all the earth, to show Himself strong [for] a people whose heart [is] perfect towards Him; (YLT)

For the eyes of the LORD range throughout the earth to show Himself strong for those whose hearts are completely His. (HCSB)

For the eyes of Jehovah run to and fro through the whole earth, to shew himself strong in the behalf of those whose heart is perfect toward him. (Darby)

Resurrection Sunday ("Easter") Today's WORD on Money™: Holiness

In his book Revolution, George Barna says, "Holiness defeats worldly cleverness." Barna defines the Church as "the people who actively participate in the intentional advancement of God's Kingdom in partnership with the Holy Spirit and other believers." He says we are not so much called to *go* to church as we are to *be* the church.

On this weekend, as we celebrate the death, burial and resurrection of our Lord and Savior Jesus Christ, let me summarize 7 passions that George Barna says were characteristic of the early Church. And by "Church", I mean the *organism*, not the organization.

1) They were expected to worship God daily, both in private, and with other believers.

2) They looked for opportunities to share the Good News through faith-based conversations.

3) They focused on intentional spiritual growth.

4) They believed that serving others demonstrated the love of Jesus to others.

5) They used their resources to benefit other believers.

6) They formed spiritual friendships.

7) They used their homes to teach their families and others the ways of God. [1]

My prayer is that we would all begin today to experience significant revival, first within ourselves, and then spreading around the world.

[1] George Barna, Revolution, 2005.

Tax Filing Day—April 15
Today's WORD on Money™:
Thoughts on Taxes

Here are some random bits of information relating to taxes:

The #1 expense paid by most American families during their lifetime is taxes.

Tax reduction is a legitimate goal. Even the IRS won't argue with that.

Tax credits reduce taxes, not income.

Know the difference between taxable, tax favored, tax deferred, and tax free.

Getting a large refund check may be a sign of poor stewardship.

Integrated tax planning is critical to long term financial success.

Tax planning and tax preparation are not the same thing.

Don't hesitate to ask questions from someone who knows. Will Rogers said, "Everybody's ignorant, just about different things."

I will say to you what I've often said to clients: "I hope you make so much money this year that you have to pay at least a $1,000,000 in taxes next year."

Mother's Day
Today's WORD on Money™:
My "Proverbs 31 Girl"[1]

For years I've called my wife a "Proverbs 31 Girl." Verses 10-31 describe her "to a tee" (except, as she admits, the "up before dawn" part!). But I also have a confession: when our children were babies, she was the one to get up at night for them about 99% of the time. I hope all of you husbands and husbands-to-be are blessed like I am with a Proverbs 31 Wife. Below are the King James and the Message translations of verses 10 to 31.

"Who can find a virtuous woman? for her price is far above rubies. The heart of her husband doth safely trust in her, so that he shall have no need of spoil. She will do him good and not evil all the days of her life. She seeketh wool, and flax, and worketh willingly with her hands. She is like the merchants' ships; she bringeth her food from afar. She riseth also while it is yet night, and giveth meat to her household, and a portion to her maidens. She considereth a field, and buyeth it: with the fruit of her hands she planteth a vineyard. She girdeth her loins with strength, and strengtheneth her arms. She perceiveth that her merchandise is good: her candle goeth not out by night. She layeth her hands to the spindle, and her hands hold the distaff. She stretcheth out her hand to the poor; yea, she reacheth forth her hands to the needy. She is not afraid of the snow for her household: for all her household are clothed with scarlet. She maketh herself coverings of tapestry; her clothing is silk and purple. Her husband is known in the gates, when he sitteth among the elders of the land. She maketh fine linen, and selleth it; and delivereth girdles unto the merchant. Strength and honour are her clothing; and she shall rejoice in time to come. She openeth her mouth with wisdom; and in her tongue is the law of kindness. She looketh well to the ways of her household, and eateth not the bread of idleness. Her children arise up, and call her blessed; her husband also, and he praiseth her. Many daughters have done virtuously, but thou excellest them all. Favour is deceitful, and beauty is vain: but a woman that feareth the LORD, she shall be praised. Give her of the fruit of her hands; and let her own works praise her in the gates." (KJV)

"A good woman is hard to find, and worth far more than diamonds. Her husband trusts her without reserve, and never has reason to regret it. Never spiteful, she treats him generously all her life long. She shops around for the best yarns and cottons, and enjoys knitting and sewing. She's like a trading ship that sails to faraway places and brings back exotic surprises. She's up before dawn, preparing breakfast for her family and organizing her day. She looks over a field and buys it, then, with money she's put aside, plants a garden. First thing in the morning, she dresses for work, rolls up her sleeves, eager to get started. She senses the worth of her work, is in no hurry to call it quits for the day. She's skilled in the crafts of home and hearth, diligent in homemaking. She's quick to assist anyone in need, reaches out to help the poor. She doesn't worry about her family when it snows; their winter clothes are all mended and ready to wear. She makes her own clothing, and dresses in colorful linens and silks. Her husband is greatly respected when he deliberates with the city fathers. She designs gowns and sells them, brings the sweaters she knits to the dress shops. Her clothes are well-made and elegant, and she always faces tomorrow with a smile. When she speaks she has something worthwhile to say, and she always says it kindly. She keeps an eye on everyone in her household, and keeps them all busy and productive. Her children respect and bless her; her husband joins in with words of praise: "Many women have done wonderful things, but you've outclassed them all!" Charm can mislead and beauty soon fades. The woman to be admired and praised is the woman who lives in the Fear-of-God. Give her everything she deserves! Festoon her life with praises!" (Message)

[1] This segment is also dedicated to my mother, Mary Katherine Powell Sappington, born March 30, 1926, died May 20, 2009.

Father's Day Today's WORD on Money™: Authentic Manhood

. . . if you're seriously seeking (truth), I challenge you to read Mere Christianity by C.S. Lewis, a former atheist and one of the greatest minds of the 20th Century . . . .

I have recently been going through a weekly men's study called "The Quest for Authentic Manhood". It was begun by Robert Lewis, who wrote Raising a Modern-Day Knight. More information can be found at www.mensfraternity.com. Men, if you get a chance, I think you will receive a great return on your investment of time in this material. I was a little skeptical when two of my friends "twisted my arm" to go. I thought that there wouldn't be that much material contained in the course that I hadn't read somewhere else. Boy, was I wrong! If you've ever wondered why you do or say some of the things you do, or why you react in certain ways in certain situations, this material will open your eyes big-time. You'll understand how many of your shortcomings came about, you'll figure out how to begin making some positive changes in your life, and you'll be a bigger blessing to your family and friends. I think almost any church would do well to sponsor these classes for the men in their congregation.

Let's talk about another man. Jesus referred to Himself as the Son of Man. When he was being tried just before he was crucified, Jesus admitted to the Jews that He was the Messiah. (Mark 14:62) It amazes me when some people try to believe only part of what He said about Himself. Because of the miracles He did, and because of what He said about Himself, He could not be just a "good man" or a “prophet”. He was either who He said He was, or He was insane, or He was a liar. Even He Himself said that in His earthly incarnation He was not “good.” (Matthew 19:17, Mark 10:18, Luke 18:19) For any of you who are skeptical about who Jesus really was, if you’re seriously seeking, I challenge you to read 2 books: Mere Christianity by C.S. Lewis, a former atheist and one of the greatest minds of the 20th Century, and Jesus Among Other Gods by Ravi Zacharias. These 2 books present evidence that I have not yet seen refuted by any skeptic. If you’re reluctant to read these books, then don’t accuse Christians of being close-minded or intolerant. As my father[1] used to say, “That’s like the pot calling the kettle black”!

Now, to all you Fathers out there—Happy Father’s Day! May you and your children draw closer than ever before, to each other and to the Lord.

[1] Richard L. Sappington was a WWII veteran, loving husband and father, follower of Jesus, and farmer. He was born December 29, 1920 and died December 15, 1994.

July 4-Independence Day
Today's WORD on Money™: "Liberal" vs. "Conservative"

. . . we can use spiritual discernment to distinguish between those who always want a hand out and those who just need a hand up.

As I write this, we are less than 2 weeks away from our 2008 Presidential elections. I discussed world views in a previous lesson, so if you're hearing this on the radio and you missed our teaching on the difference between the transcendent world view and a left or right world view, please order a copy of our book.

I once heard a Bible teacher joke about how he tried to answer people's questions in ways that would prevent them from "pigeon holing" him. He didn't want someone to boil down all of his thoughts and life experiences into one little label like "liberal" or "conservative." So he would tell people that he was liberal in his giving, conservative in his criticism of others, and moderate in his drinking! (Actually he didn't drink at all.)

As we celebrate the birth of our nation, we would all do well to listen more and stereotype less. I have a number of college friends who think I'm too conservative. I respond by offering to compare checkbooks with them. If they look puzzled, I elaborate. Far too many of the people I've encountered who consider themselves to be "liberal" are really only liberal with <u>other</u> people's money. For example, I have noticed that over the last decade, when politicians provide their tax returns, the so-called "liberals" almost always give far less to charity than do the "conservatives."

If people want to debate me about my views, and they donate at least 10% of their pre-tax income, then I am happy to have a discussion with them, because I know that I am talking with someone who puts at least some of their money "where their mouth is." But I have no time to debate people who want to be generous with someone else's pre-tax money and not their own.

Likewise, we should also be willing to expose the inconsistencies of people who call themselves "conservative." Do they put their money and their time where their mouth is? For example, do they volunteer to serve our country, or do they expect some other part of the population to carry the entire load? Do they offer to help others learn sound economic principles, or do they resort to name calling and finger pointing? Do they teach others to fish, or do they simply complain when someone asks them for a fish?

If we don't seek God's face and study His Word, we can lose the balance between "if you don't work, you don't eat" and "leave the corners of your field for the poor." Politicians take note: in the Bible, the poor had to work to gather what had been left for them in the fields. I believe this is one of several reasons why Christians have an edge over government agencies. Another advantage occurs when Christians are diligent to use the tools God has given us: we can use spiritual discernment to distinguish between those who always want a hand out and those who just need a hand up.

Scripture--2 Corinthians 9:6

But this I say, He which soweth sparingly shall reap also sparingly; and he which soweth bountifully shall reap also bountifully. (KJV)

Now this I say, he who sows sparingly will also reap sparingly, and he who sows bountifully will also reap bountifully. (NASB)

Remember: A stingy planter gets a stingy crop; a lavish planter gets a lavish crop. (Message)

[Remember] this: he who sows sparingly and grudgingly will also reap sparingly and grudgingly, and he who sows generously [that blessings may come to someone] will also reap generously and with blessings. (Amplified)

Remember this—a farmer who plants only a few seeds will get a small crop. But the one who plants generously will get a generous crop. (NLT)

The point is this: whoever sows sparingly will also reap sparingly, and whoever sows bountifully will also reap bountifully. (ESV)

And this: He who is sowing sparingly, sparingly also shall reap; and he who is sowing in blessings, in blessings also shall reap; (YLT)

Remember this: the person who sows sparingly will also reap sparingly, and the person who sows generously will also reap generously. (HCSB)

But this [is true], he that sows sparingly shall reap also sparingly; and he that sows in [the spirit of] blessing shall reap also in blessing: (Darby)

Labor Day
Today's WORD on Money™:
Businesspeople in the Bible

As we read God's Word today, it's easy to overlook the fact that many of the main characters in Bible stories were "successful," affluent businesspeople.

I'm convinced that one of the biggest moves of God in the 21st Century will be in the workplace. Around the world, God is touching businesspeople to live out their faith 7 days a week, whether they're inside or outside of a "church" building. Let's learn more about Bible heroes who were used by God in the marketplace.

As we read God's Word today, it's easy to overlook the fact that many of the main characters in Bible stories were "successful," affluent businesspeople. Usually, the Bible focuses on the spiritual lesson that the reader or the Bible character should learn from the events within the Bible story. Because of that spiritual focus, if we "speed read" these stories, then we can miss out on their applications to all areas of our modern-day lives, including our finances. Let's look at some brief examples.

Boaz is one of my favorite characters in the Bible (as is **Ruth**, for whom we named our first daughter). Not only do we read about Boaz in the book of Ruth, we learn in Matthew that Rahab the harlot[1] from Jericho was his mother, and that he was the great-grandfather of King David! In Ruth chapter 2, we learn that Boaz was a giver, and that he had compassion for the poor. In chapter 3, we see that he was honorable, and that he was careful to protect Ruth's reputation. And in chapter 4 we see that Boaz was wise, that he complied with the laws of his day, and that he was a superior negotiator. Further, he was a good steward of wealth, because he had funds quickly available to redeem Naomi's land (from Ruth 4: 9, which included all that was Elimelech's, all that was Chilion's and all that was Mahlon's!).

Here are some quick sketches of other Bible characters:

Job was the "greatest of all the men in the east", even before his wealth doubled!

Abraham was very wealthy in gold, silver, cattle; he had so much livestock that he and Lot had to part ways in order to have enough food for their animals.

Isaac sowed in the midst of famine and reaped 100-fold that year; he was great, then "very great."

Jacob had a wealth of physical and family assets.

The **Shunammite woman** was a "notable woman"; she fed and built a room for Elisha and Gehazi, and she owned land.

Esther was an entrepreneur (she oversaw a brief "catering" business!), a great negotiator, and she risked her life for her people.

David was multi-talented; he gave the equivalent of hundreds of millions toward the building of the temple in Jerusalem.

Solomon was the richest man to have lived, so far; he had multiple business interests and areas of expertise.

Hezekiah was a Godly king, and a very talented businessman and builder.

Lydia was a seller of purple to wealthy people; she had the means and the space to house Paul, Silas, and others.

Joseph is another of my favorite characters. Can you imagine being a teen-ager, believing God has told you that you will be a great ruler, and then having to wait 13 years before the dream is fulfilled? And while he was waiting, he was either a slave or a prisoner! Yet even in those lowly places, God made Joseph prosper in all he did (Genesis 39:3, 23). When we study Joseph's life, we see that our timing is not always the same as God's timing. We also see that even when we do good, we may not be immediately delivered from circumstances that we dislike (Genesis 40:14). But like the potter and the clay from Jeremiah chapter 18, if we will yield to God, he can use us as vessels—in business--to accomplish great things for His kingdom.

[1] It's my understanding that the word "harlot" has other synonyms besides "prostitute."

Rosh Hashanah (Jewish New Year) Today's WORD on Money™: Repentance and Forgiveness

My pastor recently said that refusing to forgive someone has about the same results as if you were to drink poison and then wait for the person who wronged you to die! Studies show that many illnesses are linked to attitudes and behaviors such as unforgiveness. Rosh Hashanah is meant to be a time of repentance, of "casting off" your sins, telling God you are sorry for your mistakes of the past year, and asking for help to do better in the coming year.

So this information begs the question, "If you don't forgive others, why should God forgive you?" Since Jesus has forgiven all who ask Him of the great debt that we could not repay, I urge all of us to examine our lives and to get rid of any unforgiveness that would keep us from experiencing God's best. Both our temporal well-being and our eternal destination are hanging in the balance.

May your year and your eternity be good and sweet!

Scripture--2 Timothy 2:2

The things which you have heard from me in the presence of many witnesses, entrust these to faithful men who will be able to teach others also. (NASB)

Pass on what you heard from me—the whole congregation saying Amen!— to reliable leaders who are competent to teach others. (Message)

And the [instructions] which you have heard from me along with many witnesses, transmit and entrust [as a deposit] to reliable and faithful men who will be competent and qualified to teach others also. (Amplified)

You have heard me teach things that have been confirmed by many reliable witnesses. Now teach these truths to other trustworthy people who will be able to pass them on to others. (NLT)

and what you have heard from me in the presence of many witnesses entrust to faithful men who will be able to teach others also. (ESV)

and the things that thou didst hear from me through many witnesses, these things be committing to stedfast men, who shall be sufficient also others to teach; (YLT)

And what you have heard from me in the presence of many witnesses, commit to faithful men who will be able to teach others also. (HCSB)

And the things thou hast heard of me in the presence of many witnesses, these entrust to faithful men, such as shall be competent to instruct others also. (Darby)

And what things thou hast heard of me by many witnesses, betake thou these to faithful men, which shall be able also to teach other men. (Wycliffe NT)

(This verse doesn't specifically relate to tomorrow's holiday. It's just one of my favorite verses. In fact it's become the "theme verse" for our firm. So I hope some of you will take the meaning of this verse to heart and begin to share with others some of the things you've read in this book, just as I've shared with you some of the things I've learned over the years.)

Columbus Day
Today's WORD on Money™:
Facts and Great Resources

Patrice Tsague says that as Christians, we are ambassadors with privileges. 2 Corinthians 5:20 says that we are ambassadors for Christ. Patrice's Biblical Entrepreneurship materials have some marvelous insights into what ambassadors do, and the favor that they are entitled to. I encourage you to take BE if at all possible. In the meantime, study how ambassadors operate. Then begin to see yourself as a true Ambassador for Christ.

As we celebrate Columbus Day today, I think how so much has changed since 1492. Some of the best material that I've found on Columbus is authored by Reverend Peter Marshall. Reverend Marshall has a superb teaching on Columbus, tracing Christopher's ancestors back hundreds of years before 1492. I also love Marshall's teaching on George Washington.

I don't know about you, but I don't recall any textbook stating what a strong believer Columbus was. His study of scripture was a key reason why he came to the New World. He was missions minded, not simply seeking a new route to the Orient. I think you'll be blessed by Reverend Marshall's teachings. For more information, visit www.petermarshallministries.com.

Also, as we've said earlier in our book, if you would like more information on our country's Christian heritage, study David Barton's materials, which can be obtained at www.wallbuilders.org.

Thanksgiving Day
Today's WORD on Money™:
Praise Verses

For the Christian, every day should be Thanksgiving Day . . . .

For the Christian, every day should be Thanksgiving Day, even when we encounter problems (2 Cor. 7:4). Before you read these praise verses, let me encourage you that at least once during these year-end holidays, you take both time and money to bless someone who is less fortunate than yourself. We don't give to get, but God says in many different passages that He wants His people to be a blessing, and that they will be blessed for doing so. Acts 10:4 tells us how God viewed Cornelius, who was one of the very first "Gentiles" to become a Christian:

"And (Cornelius), gazing intently at him, became frightened and said, What is it, Lord? And the angel said to him, Your prayers and your [generous] gifts to the poor have come up [as a sacrifice] to God and have been remembered by Him." (Amplified)

The following are some of the many scriptures which praise our Heavenly Father. And you don't have to wait until next Thanksgiving to read them again!

I will bless the Lord at all times. His praise shall continually be in my mouth. (Psalm 34:1)

Let them shout for joy and be glad that favor my righteous cause; yea, let them say continually, "Let the LORD be magnified who hath pleasure in the prosperity of His servant." (Psalm 35:27)

BLESS (AFFECTIONATELY, gratefully praise) the Lord, O my soul; and all that is [deepest] within me, bless His holy name! Bless (affectionately, gratefully praise) the Lord, O my soul, and forget not [one of] all His benefits--Who forgives [every one of] all your iniquities, Who heals [each one of] all your diseases, Who redeems your life from the pit and corruption, Who beautifies, dignifies, and crowns you with loving-kindness and tender mercy; Who satisfies your mouth [your necessity and desire at your personal age and situation] with good so that your youth, renewed, is like the eagle's [strong, overcoming, soaring]! (Psalm 103:1-5 Amplified)

1 Praise the Lord! How joyful are those who fear the Lord
and delight in obeying his commands.
2 Their children will be successful everywhere;
an entire generation of godly people will be blessed.
3 They themselves will be wealthy,
and their good deeds will last forever.
4 Light shines in the darkness for the godly.
They are generous, compassionate, and righteous.
5 Good comes to those who lend money generously
and conduct their business fairly.
6 Such people will not be overcome by evil.
Those who are righteous will be long remembered.
7 They do not fear bad news;
they confidently trust the Lord to care for them.
8 They are confident and fearless
and can face their foes triumphantly.
9 They share freely and give generously to those in need.
Their good deeds will be remembered forever.
They will have influence and honor.
10 The wicked will see this and be infuriated.
They will grind their teeth in anger;
they will slink away, their hopes thwarted Psalm 112 NLT)

1 Hallelujah!
Give praise, servants of the LORD;
praise the name of the LORD.
2 Let the name of the LORD be praised
both now and forever.
3 From the rising of the sun to its setting,
let the name of the LORD be praised.
4 The LORD is exalted above all the nations,
His glory above the heavens.
5 Who is like the LORD our God—
the One enthroned on high,
6 who stoops down to look
on the heavens and the earth?
7 He raises the poor from the dust
and lifts the needy from the garbage pile
8 in order to seat them with nobles—
with the nobles of His people.
9 He gives the childless woman a household,
[making her] the joyful mother of children.
Hallelujah! (Psalm 113 HCSB)

Hallelujah! Praise God in his holy house of worship,
praise him under the open skies;
Praise him for his acts of power,
praise him for his magnificent greatness;
Praise with a blast on the trumpet,
praise by strumming soft strings;
Praise him with castanets and dance,
praise him with banjo and flute;
Praise him with cymbals and a big bass drum,
praise him with fiddles and mandolin.
Let every living, breathing creature praise God!
Hallelujah! (Psalm 150 Message)

I wish you all a **HAPPY THANKSGIVING!**

Christmas Day
Today's WORD on Money™:
When Athletes Drop the Ball

. . . why do we as Christians allow critics of our faith to disparage Christianity just because Christians are not perfect?

In these times of "Political Correctness," some people are almost afraid to say the words "Merry Christmas." I believe that this type of persecution exists in part because of a double standard. Join us for a Christmas Day sports analogy.

I enjoy sports. I grew up playing baseball, basketball, and golf. Nowadays I do a variety of exercises including walking and lifting weights, in order to take good care of the physical body, or temple, that God gave me. And as a spectator, I especially enjoy watching basketball (Sic 'em, Bears and Ka-Rip, Bison . . . Zip! Bang! OBU!). But I believe that a simple sports analogy can help many Christians explain to skeptics how believers put their faith into practice. This analogy is especially helpful when someone tells you they can't follow Jesus because of all the "hypocrites"—you know, the people who call themselves Christians, but who sometimes don't act like Jesus Christ.

Anyone who enjoys sports knows that even the best athletes make mistakes. I've seen both Little League and Big League baseball players drop fly balls. I've seen NBA players call time out when there were no time outs left to call. I've seen NFL wide receivers drop a pass when no defenders were anywhere near them. So here's my question: when these players drop the ball or make mistakes, should their mistakes invalidate their sport? Should we judge a sport according to the degree of perfection that it's played, and if it's not played perfectly, should we then abolish the sport?

Obviously the answer is no. Just because a mistake was made, it does not follow that the game is flawed, or that we cannot enjoy playing or watching a game. We may enjoy it less if our team loses, especially if they lose because of making too many mistakes, but I've not yet heard of someone calling for an end to the game of basketball, even if their team played horribly. So why do we as Christians allow critics of our faith to disparage Christianity just because Christians are not perfect?

Next time you hear someone use the word "hypocrite," ask them if they like sports. If they don't, you can use analogies from many other disciplines. For example, if someone makes a mistake in math, do they stop counting? If they make a bad financial decision, do they stop using money? If you have a bad experience at a restaurant, do you stop eating?

Now please understand, I'm not saying it's OK to "let go" and yield to every selfish urge that comes your way. As Paul said in Romans 6, just because we're forgiven by the grace of God does not give us a license to sin. But I am saying that we should not allow someone to condemn us with a false standard that they would never apply to any other area of our lives <u>or</u> theirs. When we evaluate Christianity, Jesus' life alone should be our "measuring stick."

On this day when we celebrate the birth of our Lord and Savior Jesus the Christ, and in the coming years, may you truly experience the Peace on Earth and the Goodwill toward People that <u>only</u> Jesus' birth, life, death and resurrection can give you.

Scripture--John 8:32

"And ye shall know the truth, and the truth shall make you free." (KJV)

"And you will know the truth, and the truth will make you free." (NASB)

"Then you will experience for yourselves the truth, and the truth will free you." (Message)

"And you will know the Truth, and the Truth will set you free." (Amplified)

"And you will know the truth, and the truth will set you free." (NLT)

Other Resources

Books

Biblical Principles for Starting and Operating a Business by Patrice Tsague
Biblical Entrepreneurship 40-Day Coaching Guide by Patrice Tsague
Selling Among Wolves without Joining the Pack by Michael Pink
Rainforest Strategy by Michael Pink
Beyond World Class and Unconditional Excellence by Alan Ross
The Christian and His Finances by Todd Sadowski
Becoming Your Own Banker by Nelson Nash
The Pirates of Manhattan by Barry Dyke
The Church Can Change the World by Jimmy Seibert
Revolution by George Barna
God at Work by David W. Miller
God Is at Work by Ken Eldred
God @ Work by Rich Marshall
The Elk River Story by Rick Heeren
Shine by Kris Den Besten
The Shack by William P. Young
We Win! Let's Play by Dan Stratton
The Ultimate Gift by Jim Stovall
Wealth, Riches & Money by Craig Hill and Earl Pitts
Surviving Financial Meltdown by Ron Blue and Jeremy White
Money, Possessions, and Eternity by Randy Alcorn
Proof Beyond Reasonable Doubt by Mark Kelly, an online book which can be read at http://pbrd.wordpress.com/

Websites

www.twmgroupllc.com

www.lifestylegiving.com

www.moneytrax.com

www.jacobsspring.com

www.stewardshippartners.com

www.antiochcc.net

www.nacfc.org

www.provisionnetwork.com

www.okbu.edu

www.kingdomcompanies.org

www.christianmovies.com

www.infinitebanking.org

www.culturecampaign.com

www.fcci.org

www.nationalchristian.com

www.christianworldviewnetwork.com

www.garepple.com

www.nehemiahproject.org

www.samaritanfoundation.org

www.lifedirectives.org

www.wallwatchers.org

www.integratebusiness.org

www.kingdomadvisors.org

www.thepiratesofmanhattan.com

www.baylorbears.com

www.rainforeststrategy.com

www.theultimategift.com

www.jewell.edu

www.altonjones.com

www.livingwaters.com

www.wallbuilders.com

http://pbrd.wordpress.com/

http://en.wikipedia.org/wiki/Robert_Mawire

www.michaelpink.com

http://www.jerusalemsummit.org/eng/index_js_africa_participants.php

www.homerowen.com

www.innovasource.com

www.proxiproducts.com

www.ministryinsights.com

www.thefishingmachine.net

www.GossRV.com

http://www.hartmanmgmt.com

www.todayswordonmoney.com

www.timothyplan.com

www.lc.org

Seminars—TWM Group, LLC

How to Fully Fund Your Ministry in This Generation:

We offer over 12 workshops (named the "Solomon Project") designed to help churches and ministries fully fund their ministry visions. This information represents a major undertaking by our firm to come alongside of churches and ministries with tools to minister to and equip your donors. Unlike most "marketing approaches" or programs that "beg for bucks," these workshops minister and sow into the lives of your donors.

TWM Group customizes how we work with each church or ministry, based upon your needs. This may include strategic planning, individual or multiple workshops, and/or weekend retreats.

To determine your needs, we first ask for input from your leadership, and we then develop an "a la carte" proposal from which you can choose how and how much you would like for us to be involved.

Biblical Entrepreneurship:

This course is designed to help both current and potential business owners. Biblical Entrepreneurship I is a course designed to help participants identify their skills and talents, and to develop business ideas that glorify the Lord and meet community needs. One of our Certified Instructors will teach this course, using the Bible and a Biblically-based curriculum entitled "Principles of Biblical Entrepreneurship."

The course helps students learn how to identify opportunities, take calculated risks, solve problems, and exercise stewardship. Students will also learn how to develop Christ-centered character and attitude, and to understand God's purpose for profits.

BE I is the first of a three phase course series. Individuals who successfully complete BE I are eligible to enroll in BE II, "Practices of Biblical Entrepreneurship," which is a pre-requisite for BE III, "Planning a Biblically Based Business."

Godly Estate Designs:

With proper planning, many people can not only maximize what they leave to their family, but also what they give to their favorite ministries and charities. This can often also minimize what has to be paid in estate taxes, income taxes, and capital gains taxes. We offer a 2 hour seminar which covers this information in detail.

Infinite "Banking" Concept:

Find out how to create an entity that you "own"[1] and control, enabling you to recapture both principal and interest on vehicles and other big-ticket items, even if you typically pay cash for your purchases. This entity can also be designed to provide tax-advantaged income for life, as well as protection from creditors and litigation.

To learn more about the creation of the entity that you "own" [1] and control, visit http://www.mycustomvideo.com/stream/Repple.html.

Contact info@twmgroupllc.com for more information.

[1] as a steward for God

NOTES

One More Thing

Since I say in my book that our souls are the most valuable things on earth, I would be doing you a disservice if I didn't share with you how you can know that salvation is yours, now and forever. There are many scriptures and many ways to do this, but let's keep it simple and look at just 4 scriptures from the book of Romans:

Romans 3:23 (NLT) says this: "*For everyone has sinned; we all fall short of God's glorious standard.*"

Romans 6:23 (Amplified) says this: "*For the wages which sin pays is death, but the [bountiful] free gift of God is eternal life through (in union with) Jesus Christ our Lord.*"

Romans 5:8 (NLT) says this: "*But God showed his great love for us by sending Christ to die for us while we were still sinners.*"

Romans 10:9 (NLT) says this: "*If you confess with your mouth that Jesus is Lord and believe in your heart that God raised him from the dead, you will be saved. For it is by believing in your heart that you are made right with God, and it is by confessing with your mouth that you are saved.*"

So if we put the Gospel, or God's Good News, in a "nutshell", it looks like this:

Everyone has missed the mark; we all fall short of God's glorious standard. This "shortfall" is called sin. Ultimately, the result of sin is eternal, conscious separation from God and from everything good. But God offers a way to "bridge the gap". The free gift that God offers us, through Jesus, is eternal life. You see, God showed his love for us by sending Jesus to die for us. This took place before we even knew that there was a way to

escape the effects of our sins. So all we have to "do" to be rescued from eternal death is to confess that Jesus is Lord and to believe that God raised Him from the dead. Salvation, now and forevermore, comes when we believe in our hearts that Jesus alone can make us right with God. When we confess this Truth with our mouths, not only are we rescued, but then others learn of the only way that they also can have Eternal Life.

If there is anyone reading this who has not allowed God to give you His very best gift, I urge you now to do this without waiting even one more split second: Confess to God that you have sinned, and that you've come up short despite everything you've tried. Ask Him to forgive you, and then give Him permission to show you how to do things His way. It's a paradox that when you put Him first and try to live for Him, you'll actually have more peace, more joy, and more happiness than when you tried to please only yourself. Let us know of your decision, and we'll do our best to put you in touch with other followers of Jesus who can help you begin to learn more of God's ways.